Praise for
Christmas 40 Days Devotional

"As I read this wonderful, heartwarming Christmas book by Sam and Kevin Sorbo, I'm comforted that I'm not the only one who thinks Christmas is just too wonderful to be limited to only one day a year. Forty intentional days to recognize the arrival of God in the flesh to dwell among us and identify with us in the human journey. It's a reverent but celebrative series of beautiful devotions to keep the 'Christmas Sleigh' between the ditches by focusing on faith and family and how to observe and treasure every day of the Christmas Season. If you love Christmas like I do, you'll love this inspired collection of memories and devotions that your family can enjoy together. If you *don't* love Christmas like I do, then I truly hope this book will help you 'shake off' your Scrooge self and get in the true Spirit of Christmas. Merry Christmas! Enjoy it! In fact, enjoy all 40 days of it!"

—MIKE HUCKABEE, nationally syndicated TV talk show host and *New York Times* bestselling author of *The Three Cs That Made America Great*

"I've always loved Christmas. The topics in this book remind me why."

—ERIC METAXAS, host of the nationally syndicated Eric Metaxas Radio Show, and #1 *New York Times* bestselling author of *Letter to the American Church*

"With this devotional, Mrs. Sam and Kevin Sorbo have created something sorely needed in our world today. Celebrating Christmas for 40 days and beyond is one of the most glorious things a person could do! I love this!"

—JOHN RICH, country music singer-songwriter, record producer, owner of Redneck Riviera, host of *FOX The Pursuit!* and winner of Celebrity Apprentice

"There is no holiday in the calendar that is more celebrated than Christmas. The celebration of the birth of our Lord and Savior Jesus Christ is something that needs to be, in my opinion, celebrated much more. Forty days seems like a pretty good start. Kevin and Sam Sorbo have created this 40-day devotional book to honor the most important day in HIStory!"

—SCOTT HAMILTON, devoted to Jesus, and Olympic Gold Medalist

"Seeking to brighten your Christmas season? Let this devotional illuminate your heart with grace and truth!"

—PASTOR LUCAS MILES, host of *Church & State with Lucas Miles*, President of The Nfluence Network, Inc., founder of the American Pastor Project, and bestselling author of *Woke Jesus* and *The Pagan Threat*

"Whoever is jaded over Christmas is jaded over life. For such people, Mrs. Sam and Kevin Sorbo's 40 Days of Advent reflections—on Christmas and much more—are the perfect tonic, informative, refreshing, and inspiring."

—OS GUINNESS, social critic, lead drafter of the Williamsburg Charter and The Global Charter of Conscience, and editor and author of over 30 books, including *The Call: Finding and Fulfilling the Central Purpose of Your Life*

"Kevin and Sam have focused their brilliance and passion onto something so important: a call to arms for the soul of Christmas. Please read, learn, and apply."

—DALLAS JENKINS, film and television director, writer and producer, and creator, director, co-writer, and executive producer of *The Chosen*

A Loving Celebration

Christmas
40 Days
Devotional

SAM & KEVIN SORBO

— FOREWORD BY MIKE HUCKABEE —

Humanix Books
www.humanixbooks.com

HUMANIX BOOKS
Christmas 40 Days Devotional by Sam and Kevin Sorbo
Copyright © 2025 by Humanix Books
All rights reserved.

Humanix Books, P.O. Box 20989, West Palm Beach, FL 33416, USA
www.humanixbooks.com | info@humanixbooks.com

Humanix Books is a division of Humanix Publishing, LLC. Its
trademark, consisting of the words "Humanix Books," is registered
in the United States Patent and Trademark Office and in other
countries.

**Humanix Books titles may be purchased for educational, business,
or sales promotional use. For information about special discounts
for bulk purchases, please contact the Special Markets Department
at info@humanixbooks.com.**

ISBN: 978-1-63006-302-3 (Hardcover)
ISBN: 978-1-63006-303-0 (E-book)

Cover art: iStock/Adyna.

Scripture quotations are from the *New King James Bible*. Copyright
© 1982 by Thomas Nelson.

Source for hymns: https://hymnary.org.

Printed in the United States of America

10 9 8 7 6 5 4 3 2 1

*This book is lovingly dedicated to people everywhere
who have ever held Christmas close to their hearts.
May it inspire us to rekindle our collective devotion
to the love and joy that define this special season, and generously
carry its enduring message in our hearts throughout the year.*

Contents

CONTENTS

Foreword

Let's Have 40 Days of Christmas!

I'll admit that when it comes to Christmas, I'm still eight years old. I even wrote two Christmas books that were based on my childhood memories, growing up poor in a small South Arkansas town, forgetting the poverty of my youth to dream of all the things a little boy could imagine. One of those books was called *Can't Wait 'Till Christmas*. As I read this wonderful, heartwarming Christmas book by Sam and Kevin Sorbo, I'm comforted that I'm not the only one who thinks Christmas is just too wonderful to be limited to only one day a year.

You've heard the classic song about the *12 Days of Christmas*. Way too spartan for folks like us! Let's have 40 days of Christmas! And that's exactly what Sam and Kevin have given us, but not just about conspicuous consumerism and crass commercialism, but rather 40 intentional days to recognize the arrival of God in the flesh to dwell among us and identify with us in the human journey.

Their *Christmas 40 Days Devotional* is not sentimental schmaltz. It's a reverent but celebrative series of beautiful devotions to keep the "Christmas Sleigh" between the ditches by focusing on faith and family and how to observe and treasure every day of the Christmas Season.

If you love Christmas like I do, you'll love this inspired collection of memories and devotions that your family can enjoy together. If you *don't* love Christmas like I do, then I truly hope this book will help you "shake off" your Scrooge self and get in the true Spirit of Christmas.

Merry Christmas! Enjoy it! In fact, enjoy all 40 days of it!

Mike Huckabee

Preface

The commercialization of the holiday, as logical as it might be, is but a rude distraction, encouraged by all the secularist scientific developments of the past two centuries. The modern world, or perhaps we should call it the post-modern, post-Enlightenment, post-Christian society, has all but abandoned belief in anything greater than all-powerful science. Even self-proclaimed, Bible-believing Christians likely seldom crack open their Bibles, much less read them with any regularity. Our culture has been weaned of reading by an "education system" that teaches us to trust the experts. Our schooling has convinced us we need not bother perusing a book that our pastor or priest (the designated "expert") has read and is prepared to share with us.

The culture currently elevates many wrong things as if they were relevant or important. An individual's sexual proclivity is immaterial, not to mention entirely inappropriate, but icons of our culture deem it so important as to devote concert tours, news programs, and grade-school classes to it. We should not seek to harm each other, but Hollywood movies run rampant with gratuitous, unbridled violence, seeding us with thoughts we ought not entertain. Christmas has fallen prey to the cultural shift away from Biblical principles—those that would prosper us and not harm us—to the opposite.

We should tread carefully.

To counter the prevailing, materialist narrative infecting this holiday, Kevin and Sam are endorsing celebrating Christmas for a full forty days! Forty is a Biblical number—the newly released Jewish people wandered in the desert for forty years, and Jesus fasted and was tempted in the desert for forty days. Although there are Christians who believe that the holiday is simply a pagan hold-over, we choose to trust that because God gave His only son, Jesus, who certainly had a birthday, we should celebrate it! (Sam insists on celebrating her birthday for a full month, so Kevin can't really justify giving our Lord and Savior any less; can you?)

The Christmas season is divided into three parts: Advent, Christmastime, and Epiphany. I don't know which is my favorite—and why choose, right? We will label our days 1–40, because you can begin celebrating this holiday as early as October, and do a study once each week, leading up to the weeks just prior to Christmas. Our family starts decorating right before the Halloween season, as we dislike that holiday and its corresponding ghoulish décor. Our children even surprised their father one year when he was traveling extensively, by putting up some decorations and lights while he was away over my birthday! (Kevin's birthday is September 24th, meaning we started decorating more than three months before Christmas!)

For this reason, we maintain that it's never too early (and, incidentally, never too late) to start celebrating the birth of the Light of the World, for He reigns, eternally.

Introduction

Kevin Sorbo

I (Kevin) grew up going to church at least twice each week. I was an altar boy, our family prayed together, and my father led our family as a Godly man. Christmastime brought the cold weather of Minnesota and the promise of hot chocolate, cozy evenings, and sparkling mornings with freshly fallen snow draping the trees outside my window. I remember waiting, impatiently, for the network to air *A Charlie Brown Christmas*, *Frosty the Snowman*, and *How the Grinch Stole Christmas*. My mother loved to bake cookies. Her specialty were her Hershey Kiss thumbprint cookies, and I sometimes helped place the chocolate kiss in the center of the cookie, just in time to see it melt a tad on the soft, warm, freshly baked mound.

Christmas was always a family affair. Often, my father's father, a widower whose own family had boasted thirteen siblings, would spend the week with us. He always made *lefse,* a traditional Norwegian potato-dough crepe that we would spread butter and brown sugar on, roll up, and eat. Delicious!

Selmer, or Sam, as most folks called him, would make the long drive up from the prairies of Iowa to his only child who had once defied death's claim upon him. He hailed from Norway and had twelve brothers and sisters. Selmer's son Lynn grew up on the farm his dad tended, but when he was only a toddler, he fell into a barrel they used to collect rainwater. His mother found him unresponsive but snatched him out of there and had Selmer drive like heck to the doctor's. They always credited the bumpy ride in the back seat of the Ford Model T, on those bumpy dirt roads, with resuscitating him as they drove!

Christmas Eve in the Sorbo home with its five children and Grandpa Sam was the time for opening gifts, but not before going to church service at our local Lutheran church and a fine Christmas Eve dinner around our kitchen table. Our home was a modest 1,392 square feet with an as-yet unfinished basement that would later serve as my teen-aged self's bedroom. Dad installed the second bathroom downstairs, himself.

On a teacher's salary, everything about the Sorbo finances was humble, including our Christmases. But honestly, it didn't faze us one bit. All the boys had our sports and our close community, and our one sister, who split younger from older, was the calming presence in an otherwise chaotic household. We had no idea how other people lived, and we were a happy family.

A freshly cut Christmas tree with its classic evergreen scent stood harshly decorated with tinsel in our small living room, usurping the space and rightly so, drying too fast and becoming fireplace fodder. Speaking of which, stockings, made by my mother in felt with glued enhancements, hung on the small brick fireplace.

As we became old enough, the Sorbo children drew names out of a basket to determine which sibling they would be gifting for Christmas. Mom and Dad received presents from us kids and we each got perhaps three gifts from Mom and Dad.

My fondest memories were of staying up late Christmas Eve, playing with the new toys and games and my siblings. I would always try to negotiate a night spent sleeping under the Christmas tree, gazing up at the tree branches with their lights and tinsel, allowing the images to blur in front of me, and fantasizing about times to come.

Christmas morning brought the typical line for the bathroom and pancakes with syrup and sausages. Then we'd head outside to play in the snow. Our neighborhood boasted a number of school children, most of whom were my or my older brothers' friends, and we would toboggan down our gently sloping front yard and the neighbors' not-so-gentle slopes, as well. It often became a contest to see who would crash the worst.

While we celebrated the holiday as a time of joy and gifting, we also recognized it, fundamentally, as the celebration for the freedom we have with Christ's redemption from our sin and enslavement. The foundational understanding of the genesis of the Christmas holiday was never far from our thoughts, due to the deep Christian commitment of our parents. All the trimmings on tree or turkey could never diminish their reverence for our Lord and Savior, nor was it ever unacknowledged or ignored, even in the childhood antics and amusement. He was the Reason for the Season, never to be forgotten, and all our meals and celebrations began with the giving of thanks to the cause of the peace we enjoyed and the freedom we exercised to experience it.

Introduction

Sam Sorbo

I (Sam) used to struggle mightily at Christmas. It was so stressful, buying gifts for everyone, not knowing what to get them . . . what if they didn't like the gift? Money was always a concern, and fulfilling others' expectations, too. It was such a chore to go shopping with all the hustle and bustle of people rushing, stressing, and being generally cranky. And the overbearing commercialism put a distinct pallor on the holiday for me. But, of course, I wasn't Christian, so all these responses to the external holiday expressions I experienced in a spiritual vacuum.

I grew up with an atheist mother who claimed Jewish heritage, and I was sent to Saturday Hebrew school, although our household (blended with previously divorced parents, four sisters on my side and a stepsister a year older than me on my stepfather's side), celebrated Christmas and Easter because Stepdad was Protestant. Those festivities were the only expression of his Protestantism, as he never went to church, much less considered reading the Bible (that I saw, anyway.) He was a relatively disagreeable man, surrounded by us—women. I believe, now, that he hadn't realized just what he was biting off when he married my mother (and her four young daughters.)

We celebrated Christmas by decorating the tree, baking cookies, the various Christmas-y things done in school or in the community at large, then exchanging wrapped gifts on Christmas morning after a hearty breakfast of eggs, sausages, and pancakes or sometimes blintzes. One Christmas, I got a harmonica that I wasn't dexterous enough to play, and I spent the rest of the morning in bed, crying. Another Christmas when I was ten or eleven, I made the mistake of stuffing a pillow into my red long johns (the ones with the back flap) and putting on the Santa hat, laughing, "Ho, ho!" as I waddled into the living room where everyone had been waiting for me to join them. My stepfather, thoroughly frustrated at my tardiness and perhaps irked by the reason, declared, "You want to play Santa? Fine! You hand out all the gifts, then!"

Unwilling to let him see my disappointment, I passed out the gifts and laughed to cover my humiliation and shame.

So, trust me when I say, Christmas was not my holiday, until I came to Christ. Seems simple, right? Not really. Many Christians struggle to embrace the essence of the holiday spirit. This is likely because they are distracted or caught up in all the pageantry, the commercialization, and the anxiety that family dynamics often play.

We all come to Christmas from different backgrounds, but it is truly the holiday that should bring us closest together. A Savior was born to reconcile the sinner with his Creator. He came as a baby, lived a sinless life to be the example to us all, and showed us the truest, greatest love in His sacrifice for us.

INTRODUCTION

Let us approach the holiday celebration and commemoration with the reverence and joyfulness it demands, and let it unify us in our commitment to honor God as His children.

Let's dive into the *Reason for the Season,* and bring our families along for the ride, forging strong bonds and lifetime memories from timeless traditions that we establish this year.

This is the year to celebrate the *Savior.*

"For unto us a child is born, unto us a son is given: and the government shall be upon His shoulder: and His name shall be called Wonderful, Counsellor, The mighty God, The everlasting Father, The Prince of Peace." (Isaiah 9:6)

This is the year to bring your family into accordance with God the Father and His Son. This is the year to feel the *love of Christ* all season long.

Day 1

First Day of Advent

As it is written in the Prophets:
"Behold, I send My messenger
before Your face,
Who will prepare Your way
before You.

"The voice of one crying
in the wilderness:
'Prepare the way of the Lord;
Make His paths straight.'"

MARK 1:2-3

Advent is the word for the season preceding Christmas, which includes the four Sundays before December 25. It is from the Latin words *ad* (to) and *venire* (come) and can be translated to an *arrival—His arrival*, to be more precise, and so, for four weeks before that day in December known as Christ's birthday, we prepare for His coming.

It is a failing of our modern society to focus solely on the *day* of Christmas without paying much attention to the *season* of Christmas. Foundationally, this is the genesis for the heightened stress and anxiety people experience about Christmas. In fact, Christmas ought to be the time to remember to have hope! Christ overcame death! Instead, it is littered with the commercialization and pressures of heavy expectations and economic reports.

How can we shorten the celebration of that historic event to a single day during the year, and then burden it with all kinds of social uncertainty and financial obligations? These worldly tentacles on such a joyous occasion seem more like Queen Ursula of the Deep than the Prince of Peace, don't they?

Christmas is decidedly not a cartoon or a fantasy. Christ lived and died *for us.* That deserves our respect and admiration, not just an extra slice of birthday cake.

The best way to combat a cultural narrative focused on man's failings is to recalibrate our sites onto the one flawless Man: Jesus. Rather than abandon reading His story, we should devour it enthusiastically.

The Bible is the only book that reads its reader. It is not consumed; the Bible consumes, convinces, and convicts its reader. So, perhaps you might consider this little devotional a steppingstone to getting you across the chasm that culture has created between believers and their Bibles, our love letter from Heaven. And as we embark on Advent, reflect on the fact that God so loved *you*, He extended His hand through time and space, two veils that limit us but not Him, and wrote the entire event in a book, a stack of them, in fact, bound them into a larger tome, and made it available to anyone who wanted.

He is waiting for you. Are you ready to shift your focus to Him?

Prayer

Jesus, the world awaited Your birth. What a godly sacrifice, made for humanity by a man fully human, who walked this world sinless, yet accepted blame for our transgressions. What a God, the One who accomplished this incredible deed! Each year, we celebrate your birth, Your choice to enter this world, relinquish Your royal glory and don the garb of peasants, suffer our pain and humiliation and worse, bear our scars and our failings, experience even our heartaches. Forgive us for the further humiliation we bring in our apathy and detachment. Let this Advent signify my return to You! Bring me closer to You this season, that I may look beyond the world's resistance, and embrace for myself your message of hope and forgiveness. Amen.

Discussion Questions

1. Why does the culture denigrate or deny the intention of Christmas?

___

2. What other ways can we bring Jesus front and center during this time of year?

___

3. What do you think it means that the Bible reads you, instead of the other way around?

___

Christmas Commissions

1. Do an Advent calendar countdown with a child. Pick one out from the store, make one, and organize to choose it together. Explain to the child what is meant by the period before Christmas and why there are Advent calendars.
2. Send a care package to a soldier or service team overseas. Be sure to include a note wishing them comfort, joy and the hope of the Christmas season.
   - https://www.militaryonesource.mil/relationships/support-community/sending-a-military-care-package/
   - https://www.spoonfulofcomfort.com
   - https://soldiersangels.org
   - http://www.anysoldier.com/index.cfm
   - https://www.operationgratitude.com

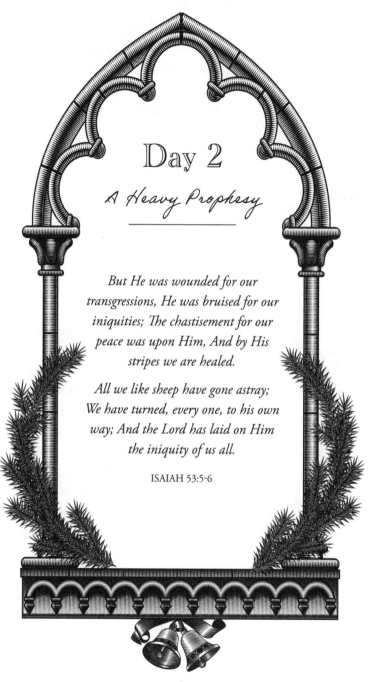

Day 2

A Heavy Prophesy

But He was wounded for our transgressions, He was bruised for our iniquities; The chastisement for our peace was upon Him, And by His stripes we are healed.

All we like sheep have gone astray; We have turned, every one, to his own way; And the Lord has laid on Him the iniquity of us all.

ISAIAH 53:5-6

The beginning of Advent, whenever you choose to start acknowledging it, should be a time of reflection of the greatest gift ever given man: forgiveness.

Note that the above passage from Isaiah was written by the prophet about 740 years before Christ's birth. Imagine being Isaiah, sitting and writing this seemingly ridiculous verse—what must he have thought, upon rereading it? And yet, he must have believed it was a message from God, and he stood for his conviction, regardless of the cost. By the time Christ was born, folks had been awaiting Him for nearly three quarters of a millennium. That's a long time! In fact, it was so long that Christ had to remind people of the texts He came to fulfill. These above lines are not the only ones that so accurately predict His earthly appearance.

According to the Apocrypha, Isaiah accurately predicted his own death, as well. He served King Hezekiah. Isaiah prophesied to the king that Manasseh, the prince, would saw him (Isaiah) asunder! Hezekiah was deeply disturbed, shouted, "Nooo!" and then ripped his garments in lamentation, poured earth on his head, and fell on his face, illustrating his own wretchedness over the anticipated tragedy. Isaiah told him there was nothing to be done, though Hezekiah swore in his heart to slay his own son to prevent this terrible injustice.

In time, King Hezekiah died, having forgotten the prediction, Manasseh became king, and his counselor was Isaiah's enemy and the enemy of truth.

Soon all kinds of witchcraft, magic, divination, fornication, and persecution of the righteous became commonplace in the culture under Manasseh's kingship. When Isaiah saw all the lawlessness and the worship of Satan and his wantonness, he withdrew into the wilderness and forswore all luxury, ostracizing himself while refusing to condone the flagrant sinfulness.

Eventually, there came an evildoer named Belchlra, who accused Isaiah and his prophet friends of being charlatans. He said that Isaiah claimed to have seen God Himself and that he spoke out against the king. Belchlra leveled these serious charges without any proof but, because evil dwelt in the heart of Manasseh, he ordered Isaiah to be sawn asunder, just like in the prediction, years before.

Before they began to saw Isaiah in two, the false prophets laughed at him and offered him an opportunity to join them, tempting him from his fear if he would simply renounce God, and instead become like a god, like them.

Isaiah, strong until the end, denounced them all. According to the account, he neither cried out nor wept, but spoke softly as if conversing with the Holy Spirit until he was sawn in two.

So many of us resent the pressure the approaching Christmas holiday imposes, and yet, reflect for a moment on the blessings in your life. After all, you don't have to live with the knowledge that an evil king has plans (and the capability) to saw your body in half!

Take a moment as you contemplate the season that is upon us. What hopes do you have this Christmas? Make a list. Write down what you've accomplished this year, including even the small things. Distill from this list a summary of your gifts and talents. Consider how you have positively affected those around you. Reflect on where your special abilities seem to be most useful.

Christmas is a time of giving, a season of extension and reaching outside your known circle, and a period of clemency—both for offering forgiveness and for receiving it. In this book, we have several suggestions for extending your Christmas impact: opportunities for you to spread the cheer and for others to benefit you by reflecting your generosity back at you.

Prayer

Father God, thank You for the blessings in my life. Please help me strive to recognize them more easily and share them more readily. Give me the courage to go beyond my known limits to help those less fortunate than me. Father, as I reflect on the sorrows in my life, let me be thankful that You are always there for me and will show me their purposes in time, for You know every hair on my head and every thought inside it. Amen.

Discussion Questions

1. Why did the false prophets ridicule and mock Isaiah?

   _____

2. How do you think Isaiah felt?

   _____

3. What does it mean that God knows our thoughts?

   _____

Christmas Commissions

1. Find a nativity scene that appeals to you. Let the children them help pick it out or allow them each to choose the one that means most to them. Work with them to imbue it with the desires of a dedicated this Christmas season, as a reminder of your destination to peace and joy. Place it in a position of prominence, so you see it when you rise in the morning and before you lie down to sleep. Perhaps this book should sit near that piece. Use it as a touchpoint to trigger thoughts of the sacrifice of Christ, first, that He entered the world and second, the reason He exited the way he did.

2. Reach out to someone you know who is lonely or dreading the Christmas season. Spend some time just chatting with them and allowing them to unload their burdens a bit.

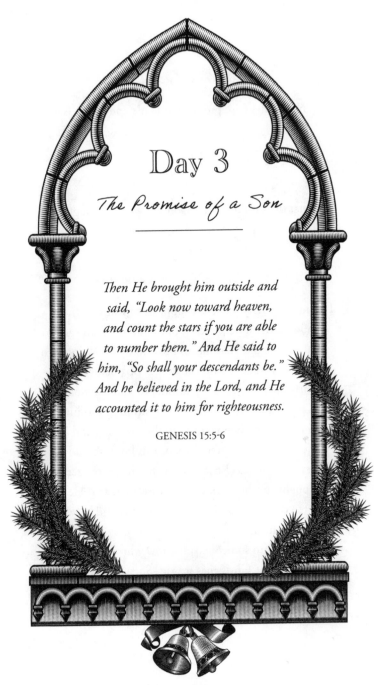

Day 3

The Promise of a Son

---

*Then He brought him outside and
said, "Look now toward heaven,
and count the stars if you are able
to number them." And He said to
him, "So shall your descendants be."
And he believed in the Lord, and He
accounted it to him for righteousness.*

GENESIS 15:5-6

When Kevin and I were expecting our first child, I got busy preparing the bedroom down the hall from ours to be the nursery. It was a project and I poured myself into it. It's no secret that we had struggled to get pregnant, so once I passed the initial morning sickness phase and was back to my high-energy self, I was determined to be over-prepared for him when he should decide to enter the world.

I made a plan, selected two colors, ordered low-odor paint, and fixed painters' tape on the walls to delineate stripes. We were expecting a boy, so I chose the old-fashioned lavender-and-cream décor to offset the plain white furniture I had ordered from a baby store. The room in our cozy townhouse in Vancouver was quite small, which suited me, and there was only enough room for the crib, changing table, and a glider chair in the corner by the single window for nursing. It would not be too much for me to paint, all by myself! I was invigorated by the impending birth of our first son!

Luckily, I started with one wall and realized quickly that I had prescribed a lot more work than anticipated to paint the entire room in stripes. So, because I was impatient to experience some success, I determined to paint each wall independently. Truthfully, I was also somewhat sceptic of my design and really wanted a good look at part of the finished product before I invested in the other three walls.

Though the anticipation of the little baby was almost too much to bear, the work was exhausting for my body, which was already preoccupied with creating life! Luckily, once I had finished the first wall and removed all the painter's tape, I realized that the stripes themselves implied more of a "prison" vibe than calm baby ambiance, so I quickly decided to paint right over them, and the room was a relaxing, single color, lavender.

I've got a photo of me up on the ladder, painting, with a large, round, belly!

Imagine having the Lord our God in conversation, like Abram in the verses above—the things we would ask Him! Would you ask him why bad things happen to good people, or what the future holds? Abram asked for a son to carry on his name and inherit his household. That was the most important thing for him, obviously, and he was distraught over the conceivable end of his lineage. The Lord comforted Abram and made a promise to him, to give him offspring too numerous to count.

Do you sometimes wish the Lord would comfort you about your future? Abram heard the word the Lord spoke to him, assuring him he would give birth to nations, and Abram believed Him, and it was counted to him as righteousness. That's all it took. Because he believed, he was considered a righteous man.

Advent is a time to prepare ourselves for the season that celebrates the birth of Christ. The first way we should make ready is with our belief, and the best way to do that is to begin with our surroundings. By behaving in expectation, with preparation for the message of Christmas that the Lord wants us to receive, we bring His Word to life in our hearts and foremost in our minds. We must cultivate an environment of anticipation, just like when a family is getting ready for the new addition of a child. Believe that Christmastime will bring great things and prepare your home to experience the joy it will bring.

We placed a large plaque with Braeden's name on the wall of the nursery, and what better way to celebrate the newborn than that? How much more should we write Jesus on our hearts and homes! To keep Him front and center during this time of year should fill our hearts with joy and celebration.

Prayer

Dear Lord, please bring me the peace that comes from knowing You. I would love to hear a word directly from You, as You comforted Abram, so, please comfort me, and prepare my ears and my heart to hear You, God. When I begin to worry, give me peace. When I start to fret, calm me. Thank you, Lord, for the wonder of Your grace. I pray all this in the name of Your son, Jesus, who came and died and rose again on the third day to defeat death and conquer fear. Amen.

Discussion Questions

1. In what other ways could we celebrate the arrival of a new member of the family?

   _____

2. What other names does the Bible tell us we should call Jesus?

   _____

3. What does it mean to write Jesus' name on your heart?

   _____

Christmas Commissions

1. Call your local fire department or sheriff's office and ask about their Christmas Outreach programs. Ask how you can be involved. Calendar your participation and schedule whatever you need to do to contribute, whether it's bringing unwrapped toys, serving food, or delivering gifts. Plan for it and see how just thinking about it brings more purpose to the holiday!

2. Tie a piece of Christmas ribbon on your keychain to somewhere it will remind you to be joyful—Christmas is coming!

Day 4

A Special Gift

For there is born to you this day in the city of David a Savior, who is Christ the Lord. And this will be the sign to you: You will find a Babe wrapped in swaddling cloths, lying in a manger.

LUKE 2:11-12

Once upon a time, there was a little boy, born in Africa to his mother and father in a lonely hut on the outskirts of a small country village. His parents named him Akiro, which means *beloved.* Mother nursed Akiro and carried him around, binding him onto her back, as she toiled in the small field they tilled and cultivated for food. Father worked the field with Mother and did some odd jobs he found in the city far away. When Father traveled, Akiro missed him a lot. Every time Father came home, Akiro was elated to see him and smothered him with love and hugs.

The boy grew slowly. He was terribly malnourished, as they were very poor, but they were a happy family. When Akiro was seven, his mother became pregnant again. The family was happy at the prospect of a new sister or brother to grow their little band.

When Mother had a big belly and was expecting the child in the next month, some African warlords came through their village, burned all the huts to the ground, and killed all the adults. Akiro witnessed the deaths of his parents as he stood by, helpless. The warlord's soldiers carried Akiro away to use him as a child soldier and train him to kill. The soldiers who had been so brutal were kind to Akiro and the other village children. They gave them candy—something few of them had ever had—and spoke softly to them.

They traveled a long way with the captive children and, assuming they had made friends of them, grew more relaxed about locking them down at night.

Akiro could never forget what his eyes had witnessed, the brutal deaths of his beloved Mother and Father and the loss of the little sister or brother in Mother's womb. He wept silently for them, for the loss of life, for the future that had vanished like mist on a lake in autumn. He dared not show his anger, but he wanted to get as far away as possible from the soldiers who had stolen his hope.

One night, the soldiers came to talk to the captives, who had grown to almost one hundred young boys. They would be at their base camp soon, and they were going to turn the boys into men. The young boys understood that the soldiers expected them to be excited about this prospect and, knowing they would be rewarded for good behavior, they all showed how eager they were to learn and perform. A few very young boys were so traumatized, they couldn't participate in the enthusiasm, but the soldiers just laughed at them and encouraged the others to talk to them to bring them around.

Akiro followed along and participated with all the celebration, but in his heart, he harbored pain and fury. He wanted nothing to do with these awful men. They were nothing like Father.

That night, he escaped! He traveled miles on his two five-year-old legs and in the morning, he found a desert road, so he followed it.

A jeep came up the road toward him. He was frightened, but realized that on the road through this part of the tundra there was no place to hide. The driver of the jeep pulled over and approached Akiro to ask him where he was from. They had no language in common, but Akiro was tired and sensed from the man's eyes that he was kind. The man had a sandwich, which he offered Akiro, and Akiro took it gladly and ate. The man picked little Akiro up and placed him in the back of the jeep, and Akiro was so exhausted, he didn't even resist, but fell fast asleep.

That was how Akiro ended up in a foster home for African boys, where they cared for him, along with many other young orphans. The staff there were kind but overwhelmed, just trying to stay open and keep the lights on, feed the children, and provide shelter for them, and had no excess love or attention they could spare for a single child. Akiro grew up there in a kind of desolation, surrounded by others but devastatingly, demonstrably alone.

One day, a representative from Samaritan's Purse arrived with shoeboxes for all the children in the orphanage. One of the staff indiscriminately handed a shoe box to Akiro, now ten years old. He opened the box and removed a toothbrush, toothpaste, a small towel and a T-shirt. There was a superball, a coloring book with odd images of cartoons he had never seen, and a small puzzle that Akiro would spend hours trying to decipher. There was also a small plush stuffed bear that was soft to the touch and squishy in his hands and a note that said, "We are praying for you. God loves you, and so do we. Merry Christmas!" Akiro couldn't read or understand the words, but the caregiver explained them to him.

Akiro cried, the tears flowing freely down his face as he held the teddy bear close to his chest. Receiving the shoe box gifts was the first time he experienced the love he felt from his parents again. It was the message to him that someone in the world—someone he likely would never meet—loved him. It was his introduction to God in heaven, who cares for each one of us with a love that is incomprehensibly large.

Prayer

Heavenly Father, let me feel the presence of Your love for me, a love that surpasses understanding, and train me to reflect that love on others with the grace and generosity that You have shown me. Amen.

Discussion Questions

1. Why do some people have difficulty accepting gifts?

_____

2. How does getting an anonymous gift imply a loving God?

_____

3. Reflect on the unacknowledged gifts in your life.

_____

Christmas Commissions

1. Pack one or more Samaritan's Purse shoeboxes. You can use any shoebox or pick up the organization's own boxes at a local church, and check for drop-off instructions, as well. The website Samaritanspurse.org has all the instructions and they deliver them. Go to the drugstore to pick up sundries, as recommended by the organization, and make a special trip to a toy store or other specialty store to pick out a special gift for each box—only ones that will fit in the shoeboxes! Take the time to write a special note to let the child who receives the box know that someone on the opposite side of the world cares about them and that there is a God in heaven who loves them.

2. The next time you eat out, say grace over the meal. Don't make a show of it, of course, but do not hide the fact that we bless our food and appreciate God's provision in our lives. Be bold in your faith and it will return ten-fold!

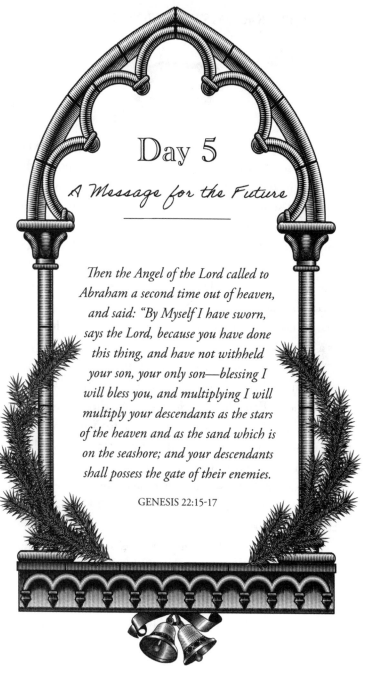

Day 5

A Message for the Future

Then the Angel of the Lord called to Abraham a second time out of heaven, and said: "By Myself I have sworn, says the Lord, because you have done this thing, and have not withheld your son, your only son—blessing I will bless you, and multiplying I will multiply your descendants as the stars of the heaven and as the sand which is on the seashore; and your descendants shall possess the gate of their enemies.

GENESIS 22:15-17

The Old Testament is full of messages of things to come. We call some of them *prophesies*, written by prophets who claimed to know the future. Many of these already have come true, and some have yet to materialize. There are also stories in the Old Testament that are intended to foreshadow, or imply, about things to come, as well as simply tell the narrative about what happened then. One of those stories is this one about Abraham and his son Isaac. Abraham loved his son Isaac, so imagine God calling to Abraham and demanding that he take his son up on the mountaintop to sacrifice him as a burnt offering!

Abraham was dutiful, gathering wood, cutting and preparing it, and loading it on his donkey. It must have been with a heavy heart that he began the task. Then he took two servants and the boy with him and set out for Mount Moriah. He must have been pondering the reasons for God's wrath in demanding his only heir as a ransom. God had promised that the boy would be his way to father the nations and people as numerous as the stars! Do you think he still had that same faith? More? Or maybe he began to doubt. . . .

After three days of walking with his servants, son, and donkey, He reached the place that God was showing him. He took a labored breath and told his servants to stay put, while he and the boy would go to worship God. He took the wood he had gathered for the burnt offering and placed it on Isaac's back, and he carried both fire and knife. What a worship that was meant to be!

On the way, Isaac innocently asked where the lamb was for the sacrifice, to which Abraham offered that God would provide the animal for their worship. God was clearly testing Abraham. He allowed Abraham to bind the boy and lay him down on the wood that was now atop the altar they had prepared. Notice that in the story in the Bible, Isaac seems quite willing.

It was only when Abraham lifted the knife to slay his own child that an angel of the Lord called out to stay his hand. Abraham had passed the test.

In this story, we see the precursor to the sacrifice God made in sending the world His Only Son. Reading about Abraham and Isaac, we feel intense relief that God spared Abraham and his son, so we might better appreciate Jesus' sacrifice for us.

Prayer

Jesus, thank You for the stories foreshadowing Your arrival. Please give me the understanding for the things that confuse me and where I lack wisdom, please show me patience. Lead me to the path when I get lost. I humbly ask You to show me Your promises that I might also believe with the faith of Abraham. Make me obedient and trusting in You alone. Amen.

Discussion Questions

1. Have you ever felt like God was testing you? How did you respond?
2. What is the meaning of sacrifice?
3. Can you think of other stories in the Old Testament that foreshadow events in the New Testament?

Christmas Commissions

1. Get or make a sign that simply says "Jesus," "Jesus Saves," or "Jesus is the Reason for the Season." Decorate it if you're feeling creative! Place it in a prominent spot in your home, so you are reminded of the coming celebration, and refer to it often with your children.
2. Visit a senior living home (bring the kids) and offer to read to someone.

Day 6

Good Things . . .

For He shall grow up before
Him as a tender plant,
And as a root out of dry ground.
He has no form or comeliness;
And when we see Him,
There is no beauty that we
should desire Him.
He is despised and rejected by men,
A Man of sorrows and
acquainted with grief.
And we hid, as it were,
our faces from Him;
He was despised,
and we did not esteem Him.

ISAIAH 53:2-3

Sometimes, things don't appear to be what they really are.

When I (Kevin) read the script for *What If . . .* I fell in love. The script was a comedy about a fast-talking mergers and acquisitions businessman who gets picked by God and put on a different path—the path God had wanted him to take in the first place. The main character had been seduced by the business world and convinced to chase fame and fortune. When he is plopped into his parallel life of husband, father, and pastor, everything goes wrong until he learns to submit to God's will.

A favorite scene in the movie is when this fast-talking mover-and-shaker suddenly must preach his first sermon as pastor of a small suburban church. The sermon is all about how God wants us to make money because money brings happiness. Talk about the wrong message! But it's the best that Arbitrage Ben can do on such short notice, having strayed long before from the Bible and all things Godly.

Years before this film project came along, I suffered three strokes that debilitated and tormented me for three years until I eventually healed. I wrote about my long and arduous recovery in my book, *True Strength: My Journey from Hercules to Mere Mortal and How Nearly Dying Saved My Life.* God seemingly plucked me from my charmed, successful, and fast-paced life and threw me into an ICU bed, where I was not allowed to move for nearly a week, because blood-thinning medicine was coursing through my veins to bust the clots that had cause the strokes.

My always-on-the-go non-stop lifestyle came to a complete halt. I watched in horror as all my dreams slipped silently away and had no idea how my life would look because my vision of the future was turned upside down. Literally, the strokes resulted in two large blind spots that impeded approximately fifteen percent of my vision.

Perhaps the role resonated with me because of the strong reflection in my own life: the main character's figurative myopia and my genuine distorted vision, his belief in career over everything else, and my dogged determination for success in Hollywood, and his eventual conversion to a simpler life filled with love and my own blessed marriage with small children ruling the roost. Perhaps I just really fell in love with Ben's arc—the transformation of the character, which tends to be the most compelling part of any role and the enticement for any good actor. Most likely, it was a combination of both. I took the part and that invoked a series of events in my life that, much like the lead character, set me on a different path, again, from the one I had long imagined.

About five years after my long recovery, I filmed the role of Ben in *What If . . .* and that experience started me on a journey of faith-based film making. I hadn't quite comprehended the impact that the medium of filmmaking has on others, but shooting this film was different from others I had done, and I had found more of my purpose in life while absorbed in its creation. The movie ultimately appealed to me because it featured a true conversion—my character brings another character to Christ. It's a poignant scene, shot inordinately well, and *What If* . . . has been a crowd favorite for years.

Would I ever have ended up doing family and faith movies without the devastating strokes and career set-back? My guess is not. But am I glad I do them, now? Absolutely.

Jesus came to the world as an infant and grew up like other small children in a relatively poor, unremarkable household. He is the greatest example of appearing different than what He was, and He bided his time until the proper moment, to accomplish what He was destined to do.

Sometimes, things appear different from how they truly are, and we must wait to find out what's really going on until after the work is done. But, oh, when we realize the truth and see the end of the story, it's a beautiful thing!

Prayer

Lord Jesus, You were despised on earth but loved us in return. Give me Your love for Your creation and show me them through Your eyes, so I can be Your hands and feet on earth. In the season of Christmas, help me be a beacon of hope for others by letting Christmas love and joy shine through me. Amen.

Discussion Questions

1. How did God use tragedy to change Kevin's path?

_____

2. When has your life derailed, out of your control, and what was your reaction?

_____

3. What techniques might we use to experience joy amid trouble?

_____

Christmas Commissions

1. Make a Christmas playlist, or just put on a Spotify pre-made one, and play the Christmas music throughout the home.
2. Watch a holiday movie together that the kids love. *A Charlie Brown Christmas* is excellent and brief, with a brilliant presentation of the Gospel woven in beautifully. We also love *It's a Wonderful Life* for its message of hope and the meaning of life. Have a short discussion about the movie after watching it. Ask the kids whether they have any questions about what happened and why.

Day 7

Angels

Though I speak with the tongues of men and of angels, but have not love, I have become sounding brass or a clanging cymbal. And though I have the gift of prophecy, and understand all mysteries and all knowledge, and though I have all faith, so that I could remove mountains, but have not love, I am nothing.

1 CORINTHIANS 13:1-3

There are numerous mentions of angels in the Bible, and most notably surrounding the birth of Christ. Angels also feature prominently around Christmastime, as a general theme. There is something ethereal about angels—according to tradition, they are beautiful, luminescent, astonishingly white, with large, feathered wings, but the Bible never fully describes them. In fact, in some instances in the Bible, angels seem to be human beings with an added "kick." Like the two angels that visit Lot in the town of Sodom.

> *Now the two angels came to Sodom in the evening, and Lot was sitting in the gate of Sodom. When Lot saw them, he rose to meet them, and he bowed himself with his face toward the ground. And he said, "Here now, my Lords, please turn in to your servant's house and spend the night, and wash your feet; then you may rise early and go on your way."*

GENESIS 19:1-2

These angels appear simply to be men, although it is evident to Lot, they are greater than your average guys, by a good deal. Is it the way they carry themselves? Is it because

31

they radiate a certain glow? We cannot know, but to Lot, and apparently, according to the story, the entire town, it's obvious. He calls them "My lords" and tries to spare them the nastiness he knows happens at night in the town square. In fact, he does everything he can to protect them from the hordes of criminal degenerates who lurk in the nights, including offering his own daughters as proxies.

Here we see a different kind of angel.

> *Then the Lord opened Balaam's eyes,*
> *and he saw the Angel of the Lord*
> *standing in the way with His drawn*
> *sword in His hand; and he bowed his*
> *head and fell flat on his face.*

NUMBERS 22:32

In the story of Balaam, his donkey could see the angel every time, but Balaam could not, until God opened his eyes.

> *And the Angel of the Lord said to*
> *Manoah, "Though you detain Me, I*
> *will not eat your food. But if you offer*
> *a burnt offering, you must offer it to*
> *the Lord." (For Manoah did not know*
> *He was the Angel of the Lord.)*

JUDGES 13:16

But later, the angel makes his nature known to Manoah and his wife, by ascending inside the fire.

It happened as the flame went up
toward heaven from the altar—the
Angel of the Lord ascended in the
flame of the altar! When Manoah and
his wife saw this, they fell on their
faces to the ground.

JUDGES 13:20

Gina was shopping in her local discount store when she noticed a gangly little girl in braids and a faded dress fawning over some stuffed animals in a bin. She was hugging a plush, aqua-colored elephant with enormous, silky ears, and exploring its floppy trunk and tiny tufted tail, when her mother turned and saw her. "Angelina don't be picking up things you ain't gonna buy! Now, put it back."

The little girl kissed the elephant and sadly but dutifully replaced the toy.

Gina had found everything she needed and, as she went to the checkout, she sneaked the plushy into her basket on the way. As she paid, the mother and daughter brought their things to the register behind her. The cashier bagged all of Gina's purchases, with the elephant last. Gina put a hand out to stop her, saying, just loud enough for the mom to hear, "That's for the little girl behind me in line."

We have angels in our daily lives, people who do kind things for us, not even for the deserved recognition. Though they may not wear wings, glow, or ascend in blazes, we should recognize the angels in our midst. Christmas is a season when angels have more prominence, and we show that

33

in our decorations. Let's use this Christmas season to watch for angels around us, give them warranted appreciation, and even try to emulate them.

Prayer

Lord in heaven, You've used angels to speak with people on earth, so I ask You to send me an angel to better hear Your voice. Let the angel speak into my life and show me where I'm wrong, guide me into righteousness. Open my eyes to show me the earthly angels in my life, and give me the words to credit them, thank them, and encourage them. Amen.

Discussion Questions

1. Describe a time you heard or felt the Lord's presence.

   _____

2. When have you been blessed by a human angel?

   _____

3. How would you feel if you saw an angel like the ones Lot saw?

   _____

Christmas Commissions

1. Clean up your street or a neighborhood park, as an individual or family activity. Bring a used shopping bag or garbage bag and pick up the trash. (We recommend wearing gloves, and even using kitchen tongs if you're squeamish.) This is a selfless act like what an earthly angel might do. Think of angels while you get the job done. You'll be surprised how good you'll feel afterwards!

2. Pray outside an abortion clinic. (Review the laws in this regard, so as not to infringe them. Ask at your church for guidance.)

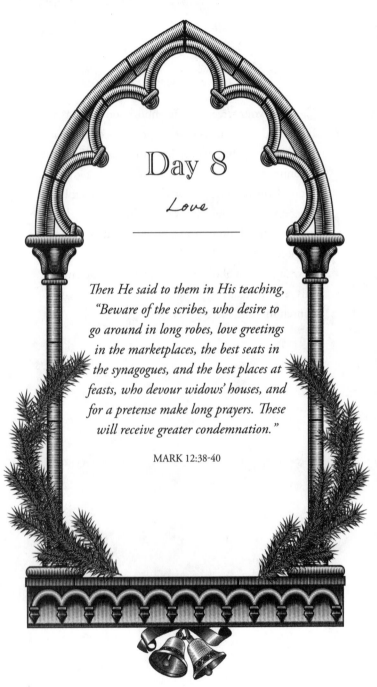

Day 8

Love

_____

*Then He said to them in His teaching,
"Beware of the scribes, who desire to
go around in long robes, love greetings
in the marketplaces, the best seats in
the synagogues, and the best places at
feasts, who devour widows' houses, and
for a pretense make long prayers. These
will receive greater condemnation."*

MARK 12:38-40

My son, when he was small, had a pair of green rubber boots. We lived in Vancouver in a narrow gray house on a slim tree-lined street. The great Northwest autumn rains inspired the lush greenery and the heavy air, fetid with the damp smell of soggy fallen leaves. One day, I parked the car down the street from our front door, unbuckled Braeden, and unloaded the bags from the back as Braeden descended from the car himself. He was getting more and more independent. There was still a slight drizzle in the air, and I needed to get inside to begin making dinner before Daddy got home from work. I had planned a nice dinner, so that required some prep, and we were running late, not to mention I was several months pregnant and need to rest.

As I watched my little guy make his way down the soaked sidewalk in front of me, kind of like a little drunken sailor, he veered toward the edge of the sidewalk, where it dipped dramatically, and water had pooled. SPLASH! Both lime green boots landed in the dirty water, and it sprayed up on his sweatshirt and into his downturned face!

He quickly pivoted to me in shock and expectation. His pudgy little hands reached up into his face to wipe away the wet grime.

I was disappointed and frustrated. He was spoiling my well-crafted (although entirely last-minute) plans! I wanted to yell at him, "Why are you getting yourself so wet and dirty?!? Now I'll have to clean you up before you go inside, little man!"

He stepped slowly out of the puddle, afraid he'd done something wrong. I checked myself, looking into his eyes, full of wonder and confusion. The day belonged to him as much as to me, and he was busy claiming it!

I slowed myself down, took a breath, calmed my nerves.

"Wow. What happened to you?" I asked in humility, trying not to smile.

"The puddle. I jump in it."

"I saw that. Was it fun?"

He nodded, slowly. Then he started laughing. I started laughing. And, of course, he jumped right back into the puddle.

I still needed to get dinner done, though. . . .

"How many more times are you going to jump in the puddle?"

"TEN!" he yelled at the top of his lungs, as he jumped.

"How about five? Can you count to five, please?"

So, he jumped five times in the puddle, and we went into the house, although much of his clothing stayed on the porch while I whisked him upstairs into the bath, laughing. God had just allowed me to learn a valuable lesson—one I would need to practice repeatedly to try to perfect. We should approach children in humility, as we have much to learn from them, like the enjoyment of life, itself.

When I heard someone explain that the parent is already bigger, stronger, and scarier than any child, so punishing a child forcibly is not an expression of power but of weakness, it brought me up short. Are we just trying to exert control when we deal with our children, or are we dealing with them in love? Children don't need to fear their parents, they need to understand their parents' undying love for them—the willingness of the devoted father to jump in front of a speeding train to defend them, and the tenderness of the caring mother to comfort them. We need to handle our children in a winsome way and allow their wonder to infect and change us.

I used to get angry when my children were unruly or ignored my demands, because they were too busy enjoying themselves or too distracted to care. Then I realized, *Why am I angry?* Because they are having a good time and I'm just trying to get my day done? When did we, as a culture, begin to begrudge children their childhoods? To demand of them they go to school for almost a full day but then after school continue to work—more than a full day—it seems almost punitive.

Think about how God deals with us, His children. He is a God of few demands. He is a winsome God, who winks at us and encourages us. He may not answer every prayer, but He hears us and comforts us when we stumble.

When we read the description of love in the above passage, let's concentrate on practicing the elements of that kind of love. If you are angry, consider the reasons. Are you justifying your own ego? At times, I was, and I needed to retrain myself.

Once I surrendered my time to my children and raised their priority in my life, I learned to jump in the puddles.

Prayer

God, please give me patience to recognize and accept when my way is not the best way forward. You've loved me so much and I bask in Your blessings every day. Thank you for being the Good Creator that you are! Help me, please, to fulfill Your purpose for me and to be a blessing to others around me every day. Amen.

Discussion Questions

1. Why do some people struggle with relinquishing the reins?

2. How could allowing others to lead bless you in the long run?

3. What does God say about those who keep the letter of the law but not its spirit?

Christmas Commissions

1. Purchase boughs of evergreens to decorate your place and bring the fragrance of fresh pine and the forest into the home. Make a wreath, or simply use them as table décor, lying down or in a vase!

2. Volunteer at a soup kitchen or homeless shelter. There's nothing like giving your time and effort to those more needy than yourself to take you out of your troubles and promote a heart of gratitude.

Day 9

Kindness

Do not be deceived, God is not mocked; for whatever a man sows, that he will also reap. For he who sows to his flesh will of the flesh reap corruption, but he who sows to the Spirit will of the Spirit reap everlasting life. And let us not grow weary while doing good, for in due season we shall reap if we do not lose heart.

GALATIONS 6:7-10

I was working my standard evening shift at the emergency room of Cedars-Sinai hospital in Los Angeles, back when I was single and working as an actress. As a girl, I had served as a candy striper in the nearby hospital in Pittsburgh and enjoyed serving others. I had enrolled in the relatively vigorous volunteer-training program. I received guidance predominantly in handwashing and performing menial tasks, but the main job of the volunteer, especially in the busy Emergency Room, was to assist and calm the patients and their families who are often in crisis. We often served as liaisons between the medical staff and the patients, for instance. Job number one was to shepherd an *unaccompanied* patient to his care room in the newly renovated ER center. Staff preferred to visit solely with the patient first, determine whatever procedures they needed, and then allow the family or friend back into the room. I remember it seemed a bit odd to me even then, as I knew patients typically depend on advocates who remember details or conceive necessary questions they might overlook. But, of course, the hospital had its rules, and I've always been a rules person.

One evening, a mother and her grown daughter entered the hospital, and the mother was in crisis. Her leg was bleeding, and although she was quiet, you could tell she was in pain. The two were dressed in worn clothing that likely had missed the last wash day, and their hair was equally unkempt.

The daughter approached me, demanding a wheelchair for her mother, and I returned quickly with one. We put her into the seat and the daughter immediately accosted me. "Listen to me! I need to go back there with her. You aren't going to separate us! You will *not* take her back there without me! Last time, we . . ." Her voice was shaking, and I clearly saw that she was stressed to the breaking point.

"All right," I said calmly, knowing this would break the sacred rule. I smiled with a soft, understanding nod.

". . . came in, they overdosed her on her insulin! Wait. What?"

"I said it's no trouble. I understand your situation, and I'm going to make sure you are treated properly. I know the rule is we take the patient back alone, but that's clearly not the case this time." I paused, to make sure she was comprehending. "Don't worry. I've got you covered."

Her face wrinkled up and she took a jagged breath in. She stemmed the tears and swallowed. "Thank . . . you," she said as I bent down and addressed her mother.

"That's a pretty bad gash you've got on your leg." I said.

She looked at me with chuckle. "I didn't even see that old crate there! Gosh darn it!"

I stood back up, wheeling her toward the triage nurse. "Right, so, we need to triage her first with the nurse over here. When you're done, come back here and when they call for her, you look for me so I can escort you back, personally, okay?"

Daughter nodded at me, incredulous.

I learned a lot during the few years that I volunteered in the Emergency Room, but the greatest lesson was the one about service. When I walked into the ER with my white volunteer coat on, I left all my personal baggage outside and began to serve others. The actor/model's life is self-centric, necessarily. It's too easy to become self-absorbed. Inside the ER, however, nothing was about me. People had terrible sicknesses, injuries, and their pain and suffering put my petty difficulties to shame. I realized how being subservient to others who sincerely deserved and warranted my attention shifted my personal problems and often, when I'd return home at around two in the morning each week, my own challenges were dwarfed and much more easily resolved.

I also learned that kindness smooths many of the bumps in the road. Kindness diffuses tempers, delays confrontations, and disarms struggles. Kindness is the outstretched hand across turgid waters, steadying its recipient to crossing safely.

Prayer

Heavenly Father, please help me to be kind, even when I'm frustrated and annoyed. Help me to see each person as Your beloved, so I stretch out my hand to them in love. Teach me to forget myself in service of others. Help me to portray Your grace and help my kindnesses overflow. Amen

Discussion Questions

1. Why do you think helping others makes our troubles look so much easier/smaller/sillier?

_____

2. Extending kindness is as easy as showing someone a smile. How do you feel when a stranger smiles at you?

_____

3. How does helping others help us fulfill The Great Commission?

_____

Christmas Commissions

1. Play I Spy with kids to find Christmas décor when out running errands, for instance, or simply on your own Christmas tree.
2. Find a local shelter and volunteer. Ask at your church if you don't have any good leads. Take a friend with you as an adventure if you're the shy type. Call first and ask what their needs are or whether there's a protocol or schedule for volunteering, so you can be better prepared.

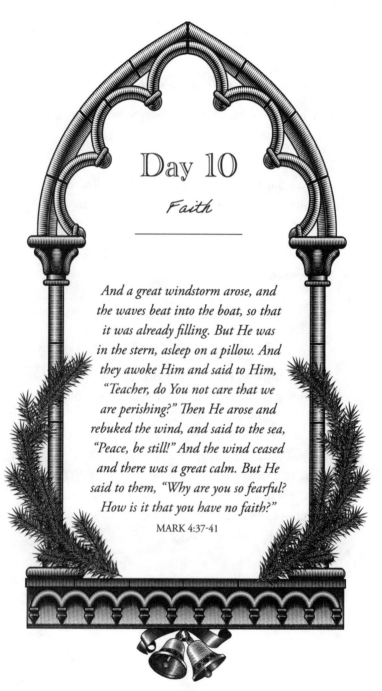

Day 10

Faith

---

*And a great windstorm arose, and
the waves beat into the boat, so that
it was already filling. But He was
in the stern, asleep on a pillow. And
they awoke Him and said to Him,
"Teacher, do You not care that we
are perishing?" Then He arose and
rebuked the wind, and said to the sea,
"Peace, be still!" And the wind ceased
and there was a great calm. But He
said to them, "Why are you so fearful?
How is it that you have no faith?"*

MARK 4:37-41

Imagine being in that boat, with the One True God, but not understanding His power. The disciples were terrified of the storm—and some were professional fishermen, so for them to be terrified, that must have been one doozy of a tempest!

Notice they didn't say, "Teacher, please calm the sea!" They seemed to ask Him if He wasn't afraid of dying. "How can you sleep at a time like this?" they posited.

After he scolded the wind and the waves, he chided them on their faith and fear.

He seemed to say, "Where there is faith, fear cannot exist."

When I experienced my first stroke, fear pulsated through me. The electrical shocks that reverberated around my brain as the first stroke hit me made the world go blurry and felt like someone had put a cattle prod to the back of my neck. Zap-crack-zing in my brain as I drove down Wilshire Boulevard in stop-and-go traffic in this rainy evening light. Streetlights and car headlights were just coming on and they all had haloes and a weird strobe effect.

I called Sam from the car and told her what had happened, as best I could describe it. I had no idea this was a stroke. Why would I? It came entirely out of nowhere and I had no reason to think I was ill, aside from a pain from my shoulder that radiated down my arm.

"I feel like I'm in an aquarium. Sounds are muffled, my vision is off, I don't get it. . . ."

"I'll come pick you up," she said, trying to be helpful.

"No. I'm still driving. Traffic is slow and it would take you too long to get here. I'll be fine, but it really was the weirdest thing, Sam."

The fear I felt initially, just from the shock of the worst sensation I've ever felt, subsided. Hearing a calm, friendly voice helped me put it into perspective. After all, I was still going to drive over to her place.

But when I got there, the residual uneasiness had not subsided. My stomach was in knots and my world was fuzzy and uncertain. Nothing seemed "right." When I did the TV interview that evening, my head pounded, and I was just going through the motions, trying to remain upright, but I wanted to crawl in a quiet hole and forget the world. I had the sense that something was terribly wrong.

The next day, I stroked in front of Sam, mid-sentence. My tongue and mouth refused to obey my speech from my brain, and I slurred. Sam's face showed astonished concern, but I still asked her, "Dih you hear at? I cah daw rie!"

Sam said, "I'm taking you to the hospital." Panic struck my solar plexus and knocked the wind out of me. And the biggest storm in my life began to rage, both inside me and around me. The squall of yesterday became a full-blown hurricane, enveloping me on a terrifying journey away from faith and back again.

I had stopped relying on God, if I ever really had. Having grown up in the church, I always had faith, but I never needed faith. Now that I needed faith, it was like a muscle that had atrophied and lacked the strength to suspend even the smallest of my cares. It took a tremendous amount of dedication, collaboration, and conversation to establish the trust connection between Jesus and me again. I went through the main stages of grief; having lost the person I had been to gain the person I became. Eventually, I redefined myself and my identity in Christ. It was challenging, and it was worth it!

Do you still fear? If there is fear in your life, try applying your faith. Try giving up your insecurities to Jesus and His eternal plan. Surrender your ego to allow Him to rule, and trust Him in His righteousness, to protect you from your fears.

Prayer

Heavenly Father, You are the author of everything and where there is faith in You there is no fear. Help me banish fear in my life and embrace Your certainty. You are above time and space, therefore You can vanquish my cares that are bound by time and space. If even the wind and the waves obey You, then I shall rest in Your goodness and love for me. Amen.

Discussion Questions

1. Why did Jesus chastise His disciples in the boat, after He pacified the storm?

2. Why were the disciples afraid, even after Jesus calmed the wind and waves?

3. How can You give Jesus more of your fears and rest more in Him?

Christmas Commissions

1. Do a quick kitchen make-over, using red or red-and-green plaid to add a festive air. Fill basic salt and pepper shakers with everything from mini trees to reindeer to add a festive touch to your table. Pull out Christmas plates or use Christmas paper plates and napkins, early.

2. Find a good place to set up doing a Christmas puzzle so the whole family can work on it together.

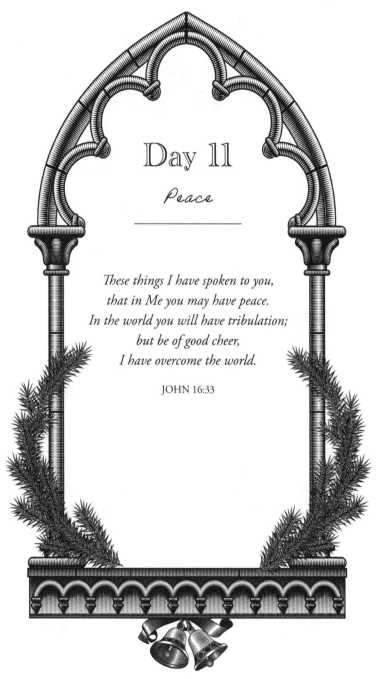

Day 11

Peace

These things I have spoken to you,
that in Me you may have peace.
In the world you will have tribulation;
but be of good cheer,
I have overcome the world.

JOHN 16:33

Every Christmas, our family enjoys watching old movies, especially musicals. *The Music Man* ranks up there as one of the finest, most enjoyable old musicals that our whole family enjoys—although we typically watch it over two nights, because it is quite long!

In *The Music Man,* the protagonist, a traveling salesman, learns that the town where he's just arrived has recently added a pool table at the billiard hall in town. He exploits that recent addition to convince all the townspeople that they've got "trouble."

Mothers of River City! Heed that warning before it's too late! Watch for the tell-tale sign of corruption! The minute your son leaves the house, does he rebuckle his knickerbockers below the knee? Is there a nicotine stain on his index finger? A dime novel hidden in the corn crib? Is he starting to memorize jokes from *Capt. Billy's Whiz Bang*?

Are certain words creeping into his conversation? Words like, like "swell"? and "so's your old man"? Well, if so my friends, ya got trouble, Right here in River City! With a capital "T" And that rhymes with "P" and that stands for "Pool."

Robert Preston played the part of the traveling salesman to perfection, but it was Meredith Wilson's writing that really made that production shine. The idea that a traveling salesman looked around for a reason to instill fear in the simple Iowan townspeople, saw the new pool table and settled on that, was inspired. The fast-talking Preston/Professor Harold Hill bowls everyone over with the speed of the words and the conviction of the coming "trouble." He whips them into a frenzy over something that may or may not ever develop into a cause for concern.

We are often seduced by mass hysteria to fear an unknown. As the audience, we laugh at the chorus of townsfolk getting worked up over Hill's predictions, but we also recognize ourselves in them.

Jesus tells us to *take heart!* By those words, He means have courage, because he has overcome "trouble" in that he overcame death. He is greater than all of it.

Courage is not the absence of fear. It is acting despite the fear.

Wilson depicts courage, or sanguine cool headedness, in the form of the attractive, tempered librarian, Marian, who is immune to the charms of this traveling salesman. She isn't simple, like the rest of the town. She is educated, well-read, and self-reliant. She refuses to be seduced into false panic over a new pool table, or any of Hill's charms, for most of the movie.

Jesus told us to have peace despite our distresses. Is it possible that we invent many of our troubles or, like the townsfolk of River City, that we allow others to fabricate them for us? Consider the things that bother you each day. Could you surrender some of them entirely to Jesus?

If you are holding two large stones and your child comes to you for a hug, you need to put down the stones to gather the child into your arms. That's all Jesus is asking you to do. Set down the stones of trouble to hold on to Him.

Memorize the verse above, so when your heart is heavy, you have a memory verse to help you focus on Him and understand that this world is fleeting, but He is eternal.

Can you practice stepping back from your ego on something that is bothering you? It isn't that you don't have a right to be bothered by it, but perhaps it simply doesn't serve you to get worked up over something you cannot change. Like traffic or the weather. Why complain? It only brings you trouble, and that was already a given, anyway.

Prayer

Jesus, please help me let go of the things that I cannot change, the things that cause me unwarranted trouble, so I can embrace You. Trouble is a given, but it need not trouble me. Help me react with a calm heart, accept with patience, and give room for joy in all circumstances. Amen.

Discussion Questions

1. How does our faith counter fear?

2. What kind of trouble upsets you most, but shouldn't?

3. What is a good advance plan for dealing with troubles as they come, to avoid hysteria like the townspeople in Wilson's musical?

Christmas Commissions

1. Make or buy some baby blankets and bring them in personally to donate them to your local pregnancy clinic.
2. When shopping, if the salesclerk seems unhappy or stressed, try sympathy and humor. Commiseration goes a lot farther than aggravation, and it feels better, personally, as well. Be sure to wish them (and everyone) a Merry Christmas!

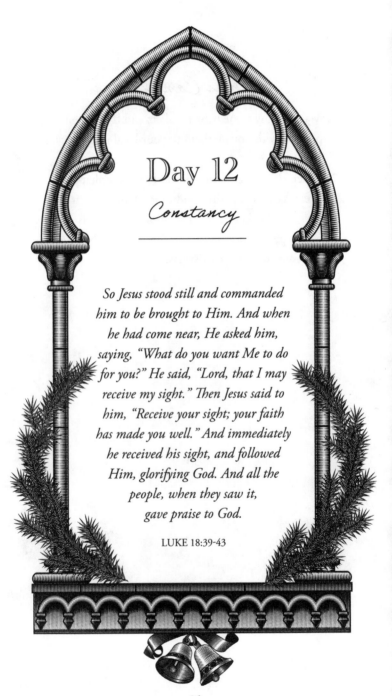

Day 12

Constancy

---

*So Jesus stood still and commanded
him to be brought to Him. And when
he had come near, He asked him,
saying, "What do you want Me to do
for you?" He said, "Lord, that I may
receive my sight." Then Jesus said to
him, "Receive your sight; your faith
has made you well." And immediately
he received his sight, and followed
Him, glorifying God. And all the
people, when they saw it,
gave praise to God.*

LUKE 18:39-43

When I was a young man, I had a paper route. (I'm *that* old!) I delivered the morning paper for my entire community, pulling down two routes in total—about a hundred homes—all by myself, early every morning.

In the arctic Minnesota winters, boy, did I want to give it up! Freezing my butt off on that iceberg-of-a-bicycle-seat, pedaling uphill in the sleet and ice, fumbling with each of the folded papers—you know, I had to fold them each myself, starting sometimes at 4:30 in the morning to get it all done before basketball practice at the gym before school.

Those were struggles, and I wanted to give up, many times. But my ego wouldn't let me. If I had a long uphill ride to finish the route, that taunted me into pushing through the biting pain in my icy lungs and the stinging burn in my thighs. My self-discipline forced me to believe I could power through, and it stood me in good stead when, years later, I faced my own mortality.

Struggling through the after-effects of several strokes, one which went to my balance center and another that affected my eyesight, it's hard to put into words all the debilitating effects I suffered, but suffice it to say that I started to understand why some people might give up.

What was going to pull me through? I settled on constancy.

This came off a concept that one of my neurologists showed us. My fiancée, Sam, and I visited the doc to ask some pretty hard questions about my life and future, one of which was about our even getting married. I was really concerned about my capability as a husband and provider, something I'll credit Sam with not being concerned about.

"What about the wedding? Should we postpone it or . . . ?"

"I tell my patients to never put off real life, as much as they can manage. Illness is not an excuse to postpone life," he said. His bushy grey beard leant him gravitas that his sparkling eyes seemed to contradict. He smiled and raised his ample eyebrows.

I looked at Sam. "See?" she said, apparently confirmed in her belief.

Dictionary.com defines *constancy* as the quality of being unchanging or unwavering, as in purpose, love, or loyalty; firmness of mind; faithfulness.

Constancy is the term I'd apply to her, in fact. She was unwavering, and as I often recount my story, I mention her strong resolve to never permit my wallowing in self-pity or regret. "It happened. Now, what are you going to do about it?" seemed to be her favorite phrase, sometimes. She was steadfast, her faith was unwavering, her support was committed, and for that I'm grateful.

It took me a while to see through the veil of my stroke-induced deficits, but I decided that they didn't change my core; they just changed how I interacted with life, and I determined to battle back to how it used to be. So, I couldn't work out in the gym like I used to—I decided that would be my goal to work back toward. So, I couldn't go out to a restaurant without a total brain melt when I returned home and the following day (migraine, nausea, dizziness, and inability to engage on any level). I vowed to battle back to as close to normalcy as possible.

I remained constant to my goals, and eventually achieved them.

In the Bible story above, we see Jesus being constant. He never changes, allowing a man others scolded to come to him and ask for healing. He gives freely to those who believe.

Prayer

Heavenly Father, You are constancy itself. Give me the peace to remain constant even in changing times. In constancy is strength, solidity, and stalwartness. I want to be sturdy to weather any challenges, and through You, I know I can achieve that. Help me to be and remain consistent and persevere. Amen.

Discussion Questions

1. When Jesus says, "Your faith has healed you," what does He mean?

_____

2. How important is it to have reliable people around you?

_____

3. When have you powered through to achieve, even though you wanted to quit?

_____

Christmas Commissions

1. Hang ornaments from the ceiling or hanging light fixture. Get small oranges or clementines and a jar of cloves (from the spices section of the supermarket). Stick the cloves into the oranges so they look a little prickly. Place in a bowl lined with greenery, or tie with ribbon and hang over your kitchen sink or from the hanging fixture over your table, for a pretty, scented decor.

2. Make Christmas sugar cookies and decorate them. Gift cookies to friends, service providers, or coworkers.

Recipe:
1 cup granulated sugar
1 cup powdered sugar plus some for dusting
1 cup butter
0.5 cups canola oil
2 eggs
4.5 cups sifted flour
1 teaspoon cream of tartar
2 teaspoon vanilla extract
2 teaspoon cinnamon

Beat butter and sugars until light and airy. Add the oil and beat in until combined. Add eggs and vanilla. Sift together all dry ingredients and add while beating into the wet mixture. Chill for 30 minutes before rolling out in portions to about 0.25 inches thick. Use some fun, ample-sized Christmas cookie cutters and carefully transfer to greased baking sheets. Dust with powdered sugar before baking. Bake at 375 degrees for 10–12 minutes, until the edges are slightly brown.

For the royal icing, which you may color in portions, mix 1 pound of powdered sugar, 5 tablespoons meringue powder, and 1 teaspoon vanilla, or to taste. Peppermint or other flavors can be fun for variation! Add a scant 0.5 cups of water until it's the thickness you like.

Once the cookies are cool, use plastic bags with tips cut or icing bags with special tips, various Christmas-themed sprinkles and candies, and colored sugars or crushed candy canes, to decorate.

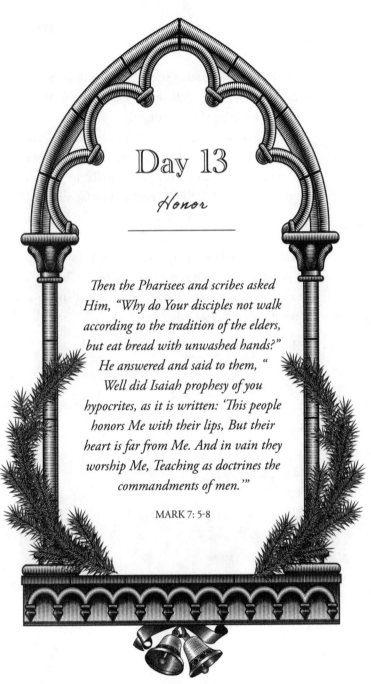

Day 13

Honor

Then the Pharisees and scribes asked Him, "Why do Your disciples not walk according to the tradition of the elders, but eat bread with unwashed hands?" He answered and said to them, " Well did Isaiah prophesy of you hypocrites, as it is written: 'This people honors Me with their lips, But their heart is far from Me. And in vain they worship Me, Teaching as doctrines the commandments of men.'"

MARK 7: 5-8

Sandy struggled with the Christmas season. She observed skeptically as her local mall transformed, just after Halloween, into the predominantly red and green of Christmas, with a few touches of the blue and white of Channukkah.

It all seemed so perfunctory. People were just going through the motions, she thought.

The day boasted an early-winter overcast frozen drizzle. Nobody should be out in that, but Sandy needed to get a jump on all the decorating and shopping and cooking in front of her. Her two grown children would be coming to the house for the holiday and their little children (her beloved, precious, grandbabies) expected the festive tree, presents, and her homemade cookies, but since before the finalization of her drawn-out divorce the previous year from her long-cheating husband, the holiday seemed to metamorphose into a heavy time of melancholy and resentment.

Sandy begrudgingly drove to the mall to pick up some of what was on her very long "to do" list. In the packed mall parking lot, she found a space about as far from the entrance as possible. What a chore! She'd be much happier at home in a warm bath with a glass of wine. Perhaps she'd draw one after dinner tonight.

She parked the car and pulled out her umbrella, tucking her purse in close to her side so it wouldn't get wet. As she started the trek toward the large, festively decorated entrance, she trudged past a minivan, where a gal was wrestling someone into a wheelchair. The driver's purse caught on the handle of the chair and spilled its contents onto the ground. A lipstick rolled under the car, a wallet flew in the opposite direction, and other papers and paraphernalia landed in the mucky, snowy sludge.

"Oh, darn it!"

Instinctively, Sandy bent down to help retrieve the escaping items.

"Thank you so much!" the woman gushed, juggling open an umbrella that also had fallen. It sprayed dirty water onto Sandy's coat. "Oh! I'm so sorry! I'm so clumsy!"

"Ah, what a day, huh? Why are we even battling the elements, today, right?"

"We couldn't miss this . . ." the man in the wheelchair interjected.

"No!" the woman agreed, handing the umbrella to him and ducking under it while stuffing everything she had retrieved back into her purse and taking the papers from Sandy, as well.

"Our niece is singing in a choir inside the mall in an hour," the gentleman elaborated.

"How exciting for you," Sandy said.

"Where are my manners?" It was a rhetorical question. "Why don't you join us for the brief performance? It's open to everyone. Thank you for stopping to help. It was very kind. And I repaid you by spraying your jacket. Let me buy you a coffee?"

"That's not necessary. . . ."

"Of course it isn't," she laughed, cheerily, "but I'd like to, anyway. It's the season."

"Don't try to talk her out of it," the man interjected as his wife wheeled him down the glistening blacktop. His laugh turned into a rough cough.

As they waited at the children's concert, Sandy sipped her warm coffee and took in all the bright, colorful decorations surrounding her. Theresa had explained that her husband's illness had left him too weak to walk far, and she hadn't yet mastered wheelchair transfers, but for their adored niece, they would battle any elements! Plus, her husband loved touring the mall to gawk at all the cheerful Christmas window dressings.

Sandy's thoughts drifted naturally to her own children and their young ones. If they were performing in a concert, would she brave wind and rain to be there? Would she resent the imposition?

As the November weather dripped off her coat, Sandy felt her heart thaw a bit as well. It could always be worse, she reasoned. Resenting the holiday was no way to go through life, she decided. She resolved to reset her spirit to appreciation, made a breakfast date with her new friends as they waited, and sent a prayer of thanks to God for showing her the errors in her resentfulness.

Prayer

God, show me where I misstep. Let me see through Your eyes, to appreciate what I have and cherish Your precious gifts. I praise You and Your wonderful creation. I honor Your Holy Name. Amen.

Discussion Questions

1. If you are resentful of something in your life, is it time to release that burden and allow God to work in your heart?

   _____

2. We often fail to see God's hand in the everyday. Name a recent time where in hindsight, you found Him.

   _____

3. Look for someone who is struggling and find a way to reach out in a generous gesture of kindness.

   _____

Christmas Commissions

1. Make a stovetop potpourri—Ah! The smell of fruity/cinnamon/spice goodness throughout the house!
2. Find or decorate personalized Christmas stockings for the family or friends. Fill them with stocking stuffers like games or prizes, small oranges, chocolates, and other Christmas goodies.

Day 14

Seeking

O God, You are my God; Early will I seek You; My soul thirsts for You; My flesh longs for You In a dry and thirsty land Where there is no water.

PSALM 63:1

When Bella was a little girl, her grandmother gave her a Bible for Christmas. She also got a harmonica, a sweater, socks, and some Pop Rocks (her favorite candy). Her older sister, Ruby, gave her a scarf, which she thought was cool, but it didn't satisfy her youthful desire for toys. She had anticipated that at least Gammy would provide some fun with her gift, but the small Bible, with its pink, fake-leather cover and tiny writing, was the last thing on her wish list.

After all the presents were opened and Christmas "dinner" (at lunchtime) was concluded, Bella was left to her own devices. She went to her room in Gammy's old house that she shared with Gammy, Ruby, and Mom, and threw herself on the bed to try the harmonica. It made a horrible sound when she blew through it. She tried both ways, blowing in and out, having read the basic instructions. It sounded even worse.

She had heard talented people play the mouthorgan, but for the life of her, she couldn't get her togue to twist in the way indicated by the flimsy, folded flyer in the red case. Her attempts were half-hearted because she was so disappointed with the rest of her Christmas gifts and the fact that her mother had failed to make her typical yummy yams with marshmallows and had made creamed spinach, instead! (Who does that?!)

She carefully opened a packet of Pop Rocks and poured some on her tongue, savoring them as they fizzled. When they had finished, her disappointment overwhelmed her.

She fell back onto her pillow and cried, mumbling, "Stupid harmonica! Stupid Christmas! Stupid, dumb gifts! I'll never learn to play this thing."

Suddenly, there was a soft knock at the door, and it opened a crack. Gammy stood in the doorway, her stooped shoulders making it look like she lacked a neck. She had a smile on her face that faded as she asked, "Bella, are you crying?"

Bella reflexively wiped her eyes, shaking her head "No," as a fresh batch of tears poured forth. Her face scrunched up despite all attempts to calm herself.

Gammy shut the door behind her and sat facing Bella on her bed, stroking her cheek, asking, "What are you sad about?"

Bella shrugged her shoulders. How could she put into words her sadness and avoid the conviction of her selfishness?

"You know, people take years to learn how to play the mouth harp. It isn't something you can just pick up and play. You know how long I've been playing the piano, and I'm not even that good—yet!"

"So, I just have to practice, like on piano . . ." she said stoically, through a ragged sigh. She felt guilty and wished her grandma would just leave her to her misery. It was more satisfying to feel sorry for herself.

"Belle-belle, Christmas is about so much more than the presents. It's about drawing closer to God, feeling His presence."

"I know. It's about Jesus' birthday," she answered quickly.

"That's right. Now, you still don't know why you're sad?"

Bella thought about it for a minute. "I'm just frustrated with the harmonica, Gammy," she lied.

Gammy looked at her and Bella felt like she saw the untruth. She breathed deeply and said softly, "Okay, well, I want you to know that the reason I gave you that Bible is because one day, maybe soon or maybe not for a long time, you will need to look for answers. That book has all the answers you will ever need."

"Thank you, Gammy," Bella answered. She loved Gammy but the comfort Gammy offered didn't satisfy her. Bella preferred to just be miserable, right then.

At thirty-four, Bella had a high-powered career as an investment banker. She drove a sweet cherry red sports car and went on vacations to spa resorts to be pampered, when she did take time for herself. She hadn't gotten married and struggled to even keep a serious relationship because she worked such long hours and was forever cancelling dates at the last minute.

Bella lived the successful life everyone aspired to, and she was often pleased, but never satisfied. True happiness eluded her. One Sunday evening as she walked into her bedroom, the framed picture of her late grandmother seemed to beckon to her as she walked past. She had missed Gammy's funeral for a conference where she was keynote speaker and couldn't shake the nagging guilt. It was a justified absence, so why did she feel so bad about it? Gammy was dead—she didn't know Bella wasn't there. And everyone else had told her they understood. Bella picked up the photo, looking into the eyes of the one who loved her unconditionally. She missed Gammy.

"Spilt milk, Belle-belle," Bella said to herself. A tear escaped her eye and drifted slowly down her cheek.

Suddenly, Bella dashed to her closet and pulled down the old dusty memories box from the top shelf. She unfolded the top flaps and moved out layers of a sweatshirt, some books and papers, and a small trinket box. Finally, she saw it—the red harmonica box. Next to it was the pink Bible that she had stowed away and forgotten about.

She pulled out the Bible and held it reverentially, one hand under and the other on top. She had just remembered where to find what she was missing.

Prayer

Father in heaven, stay in my presence. Shine Your face upon me and allow me to feel Your desire for my life. Help me pursue You and encourage me to turn to You for guidance. Thank you for always being there for me. Now help me remember and heed your strong counsel. Amen.

Discussion Questions

1. Why did God cause the Bible to be written?

_____

2. When have you had to ask for forgiveness?

_____

3. Did it feel better or worse after you were forgiven?

_____

Christmas Commissions

1. Go to the craft store and get a pack of clear plastic ornaments. Get glitter, acrylic paint, brushes etc. Google images to get inspiration for decorating them as a group activity. Serve hot cider and Christmas cookies. Consider having a theme or a color scheme.
2. Show others you care about them by asking how they are doing and really listening to their answers.

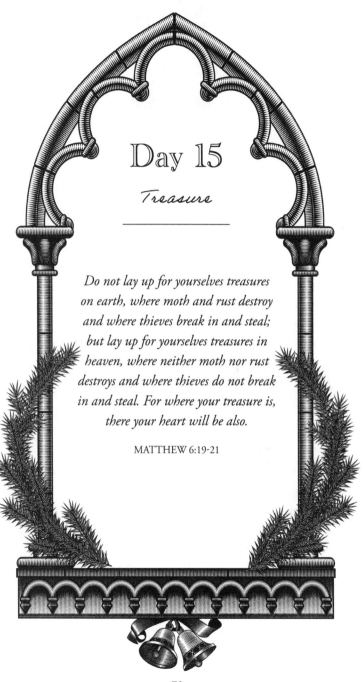

Day 15

Treasure

---

*Do not lay up for yourselves treasures
on earth, where moth and rust destroy
and where thieves break in and steal;
but lay up for yourselves treasures in
heaven, where neither moth nor rust
destroys and where thieves do not break
in and steal. For where your treasure is,
there your heart will be also.*

MATTHEW 6:19-21

"Even *Jesus* was a socialist!" Catherine said, exasperated. She and her best friend were having one of their impassioned discussions about politics, and Catherine had just pulled out the trump card—invoking Christ as final arbiter.

Angie leveled a stern gaze at her wayward sixteen-year-old friend. "No, Cat, He wasn't, and I can prove it to you."

"Really!" Cat was not about to be convinced, but her mother seemed so determined, she decided it might be fun to watch her crash and burn. After all, in church, their youth pastor had basically made the case for surrendering all your worldly possessions and living only for Jesus. It didn't really make sense to her how one was supposed to do that, but the story about the guy asking Jesus what he could do was clear. Jesus told him to sell all his belongings, which Jesus then considered would be harder than for a camel to fit through the eye of a needle!

Angie said, "Do you remember the parable of the talents?"

Cat rolled her eyes. "Of course I do!"

"Okay, so, what happened to the guy with five talents?"

"He used them and turned them into double what he'd been given. So what?"

"So, the only way he could've done that is not *using* them, but investing them, right?"

"Okay, sure, but I don't see where you're going with this."

Angie smiled. "You will; trust me. So, the second servant. What happened to him, then?"

"He was given only two talents, but he also turned them into four, so the master told him he had done well."

"In fact, his master told him and the first one both that he would put them in charge of many things. He would reward them further, for investing well, right?"

"Yeah," agreed Cat. "That's right, but the third servant was only given one talent."

"According to his ability, remember? They each received according to their abilities."

"Yes, I know. And the third servant had buried his talent in the ground for safe-keeping."

"So, he came back with only what his master had originally entrusted him with, right? But do you remember what he says to his master before he hands him back his money? He says, 'I knew you to be a hard man, harvesting where you have not sown and gathering where you haven't scattered seed.' He tells the master that he was too afraid to do anything but bury the talent underground! And what was his master's reaction to that?"

"Something like 'You wicked, lazy servant!' right?"

"Exactly. The master was angry either because the guy was so rude or because he had failed to invest wisely! Either way, he took the one talent and gave it to the one who already had ten and he threw the worthless servant out on his bum."

"Okay, fine, but I don't see how this proves that Jesus wasn't a socialist," challenged Cat.

Angie smiled again. "Cat, the master—in this case, God—honors those who multiply their wealth, to the point of blessing them even *more,* and he takes away the blessings from misers who just cling to their wealth. That's capitalism—in the Bible."

Cat looked at her mother. She searched for a rebuttal. "Wait . . . But Jesus told the rich guy to sell all his belongings . . . ?"

"Yeah, but that doesn't mean he didn't like wealth—which is the claim of every socialist. He said that, but only after the young man said he'd done everything else perfectly, like keeping all of God's commandments. The man asked Jesus what he lacked, and that's when the Lord hit upon the exact Achilles' heel of this guy—his wealth. It was the one thing this rich guy couldn't part with. His riches were his idol, before God, so the prescription was for *him* and others who worship money, not for the world. If God loves socialism, why does He tell us He means to prosper us? Everyone knows that socialism is the opposite of prosperity."

Cat seemed a bit alarmed. "What do you say about the verse 'Do not store up treasure on earth, or whatever?"

"Yeah," Angie agreed, "That's a good question. But remember the ending of that verse is that wherever your treasure is, your heart is there. So, I think the admonition is to beware of coveting wealth, for itself, because *then* you'll be like the rich young man, worshipping money. Make sure you are living for Christ in all that you do, but you don't have to run away from money, either."

Cat considered this a moment, and realized she felt convicted, but in a good way. "You're not too shabby, Mom," she said, smiling.

Prayer

Lord, give me wisdom with my finances. Lead in truth and trust, Lord, for Your provision, instead of in Man's. In Man's world we've accepted that money is the highest value, but I want Your values, instead. Give me the courage and the grace to pursue Your desires for my life. Show me the way, please, this Christmas. Amen.

Discussion Questions

1. Why is it so difficult for the young rich man to follow Jesus?

2. Why do many Christians find socialism so appealing?

3. How does God create wealth on earth?

Christmas Commissions

1. Bake or buy cookies or snacks and deliver them to the local fire department, police station, or nursing home.
2. Find an attend a local Christmas performance.

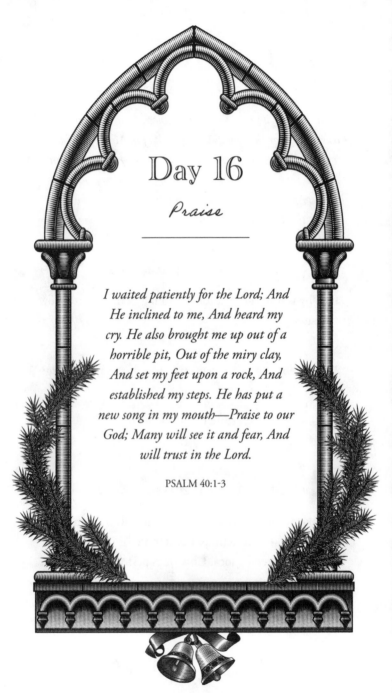

Day 16

Praise

---

*I waited patiently for the Lord; And
He inclined to me, And heard my
cry. He also brought me up out of a
horrible pit, Out of the miry clay,
And set my feet upon a rock, And
established my steps. He has put a
new song in my mouth—Praise to our
God; Many will see it and fear, And
will trust in the Lord.*

PSALM 40:1-3

My head was pounding. I couldn't sleep. The lightning flashes inside my eyelids, like static electricity from a generator, pulsated, unnerving me. I let out a deep breath, trying to calm my nerves. A sense of foreboding hung over me like the stench of old garbage. I got out of bed and paced the room until the idea hit me to ascend the stairs to the roof of the six-story building where I was staying in Los Angeles.

It had been only two weeks since my discharge from Cedars-Sinai Hospital, which was only blocks away. Some might find it a consolation in the case of another emergency, but I found it eerie, never wanting to set foot back in that place. They had diagnosed me with strokes from a shoulder aneurism, simple words to describe devastating effects. They treated the aneurism and told me the strokes were contained. The neurologist even told me to get back to work if I wanted.

I wanted to go back to work as if nothing had happened. If only.

My brain literally couldn't handle it. I had collapsed on set and paramedics had carried me out on a stretcher. After another MRI at the emergency room in Atlanta, the doctor there confirmed the strokes and the subsequent brain damage. He had looked at me like I was a bit wacky, to even think of working in my brain-damaged "condition."

So here I was, back in LA with my tail between my legs. Giving up was never my move. I persevere just for the sake of not quitting. I'm competitive, always striving, eternally motivated. But now . . . now I was at a loss, and I didn't like the feeling.

The air up on the roof was cool and the night was dark, save for the city lights reflected through the sky. I walked around the perimeter where a white wall-barrier kept visitors from approaching too closely the edge of the building and I stopped at a spot to look out across other rooftops to the taller buildings farther away. The soft cacophony of gentle traffic wafted up to me as the shimmering distant buildings competed with the stars above.

I took in the scene, but it all seemed grimly tainted, somehow. I put my elbows on the wall and leaned forward, searching but not finding. What was I looking for? My pulsating headache hadn't abated, and my vision wasn't right. I wavered, dizzy and off-balance—another effect of the strokes. I felt frustrated and apprehensive, but not from some concrete thing. Mostly I was very, very sad. Tears streamed slowly from my eyes. I realized I was mourning a great loss, and that night, on the rooftop in the cool southern California night air, I knew it was the loss of the person I had been, before my strokes.

I was no longer Kevin Sorbo—not that guy. Like an undercover agent whose identity has been compromised, I needed to find a new ID. My problem was that I couldn't just make it up. It was like my face had been blurred out, so I couldn't recognize myself in the mirror anymore. People could still call me by that name, but the old Kevin was gone and buried under a mountain of treatments, medical bills, prescriptions, and relentless symptoms. Those things also didn't define me, but they sure eclipsed the OG.

I prayed on the roof to a God who seemed uncaring and remote. I begged Him to fix me—put me back together like I had been before. Turn back the clock, make it like it never happened, or at least restore what I'd lost. I didn't think He would, but I pleaded my case.

I was so broken I didn't even know where to start the healing process. I was blessed with good guidance on my recovery journey—and that's what it was, a three-year journey with ups and downs and blind curves. I eventually realized those blessings, many of them coming just at the "right" times, were the contributions of a loving and creative Abba in heaven. I turned my face to Him repeatedly and He heard my cries. He changed the course of my life through the tragedy of my strokes, but set my feet on firmer ground and directed my course into foreign lands. When I read the Psalm above, I realize it was written for my life.

Perhaps it was also written for yours. Maybe you are not yet calling out to Him to set your feet on solid ground, but He will if you ask earnestly from your heart.

Prayer

Heavenly Father, thank you for solid ground to walk on. Thank you for directing my path, for hearing my cry, for lifting me up. Search my heart. Show me any errors in my walk. Cleanse my mind of impure thoughts and turn my eyes toward You. I praise You and Your powerful way in my life. Amen.

Discussion Questions

1. Psalms is full of lamentations. What does God think of us complaining to Him?

2. What was a time when you cried out to God?

3. How can you be the one whom God uses to help someone else?

Christmas Commissions

1. Buy and wear matching family PJs.
2. Make Christmas tree shaped pancakes for breakfast or decorate round pancakes like wreaths with berries and green whipped cream.
3. Use Christmas cards as décor. Hang them from twine across the mantel or from a ceiling light fixture.

Day 17

Endurance

---

*Therefore we also, since we are
surrounded by so great a cloud of
witnesses, let us lay aside every weight,
and the sin which so easily ensnares us,
and let us run with endurance the race
that is set before us, looking unto Jesus,
the author and finisher of our faith,
who for the joy that was set before
Him endured the cross, despising the
shame, and has sat down at the right
hand of the throne of God.*

HEBREWS 12:1-2

"It doesn't matter if you win or lose . . . it only matters how you play the game." That's an adage that we often hear and discount. *Of course, it matters if you win!* we think. Why play if you don't want the win? But in the long run, the way you play the game—any game—defines your character, and character is always more important than accolades.

Evan and Mikey had been friends since childhood. They grew up together, spending lots of time at one's house or the others. It came as nobody's surprise when they eventually starting a carpet-cleaning business together.

The boys worked long hours, but they ran their own schedule, which gave them enough free time to enjoy life a bit, and their business steadily grew. Mikey was the charming one who could talk people into hiring them just for the entertainment value. Evan was the hard-working and meticulous one, staying on point until the final stain came out. They each had a favorite saying that encapsulated their personalities. Evan was driven by truth, and Mikey focused on having fun.

It was late in the mid-December day when the call came on Evan's cell phone. His dad had been diagnosed with renal failure. He would need dialysis twice each week and someone to be with him for the four or so hours each time, Evan's sister told him, and she was traveling for the holiday to visit her husband's family. Evan knew her too well to even try to negotiate with her.

Evan had a serious conversation with Mikey—the kind Mikey least enjoyed. He explained the situation and then asked, "How can I work my schedule around my taking my dad twice a week for his dialysis? It's Christmas and we have tons of bookings."

Mikey met Evan's gaze with his cool easy calm. "No biggie," he said, smiling. "We can make up for the lost weekdays with our weekends."

Evan grew frustrated. "Is there nothing that fazes you at all? My dad, who you know well, just got diagnosed with kidney failure. He's gonna need a new kidney, Mikey, and you're taking it like it's just another day in the park."

Mikey grew more serious. "Evan, it *is* another day in the park—during a blizzard. But we're still in the park. Listen, I agree this is terrible news. Is that what you're looking for? A pity party? Because I find those to be wastes of time."

Evan got up, the weight of the moment bearing down on him. He ran his fingers through his hair, his go-to gesture to relieve tension. Evan's mother had passed away the year before and he was reliving much of his grief and stress over her loss.

"Do you want me to work alone, instead? Without you?"

"Mikey, you know you don't have the attention to detail this job requires to keep the referrals coming."

"Oh . . . so, now you're insulting me?" Evan wasn't looking at Mikey to see his smirk.

Evan shrugged morosely. "Truth is truth." That was his go-to phrase.

Mikey quickly countered his negativity, "You know what I think? I think you're scared, and you're taking it out on me.

And there's nothing I can do to fix this but work to make your life a bit easier. And . . . you're right. I don't focus on details like you do. That's why we are a great team. Mikey, this is a challenge in life. We will get through it because we can't go around it. It's just that simple. So, make the choice to appreciate the view as you travel. Perspective is everything and joy is joy."

"Easier said than done," Evan responded morosely.

Paul's first day of dialysis was a few days later. The boys had cleared the work schedule for that day. Mikey insisted on accompanying them, naturally. He'd known Paul his whole life.

Tired Christmas decorations hung limply on the walls, but that didn't deter Mikey's spirit. His carefree, joyful demeanor gave everyone in the clinic a boost. He had brought candy to share, and a few magazines, allowing Paul to choose first, but then offering the rest to others and commenting glibly on their choices. Pretty soon, the people were conversing, first over the magazines but soon a general conversation erupted. Even the nurses noticed and enjoyed themselves more.

When the guys were getting ready to leave, the nurses thanked Mikey for brightening everyone's day.

"We have to do what we can with what we have," he said.

Evan clapped him on his back. "Truth is truth!"

Mikey didn't even look up. "And joy is joy."

Evan smiled and shook his head. He'd been pig-headed before, when the diagnosis was fresh and stinging, but now he understood Mikey's strategy. The only way out was through, and perspective meant everything.

Prayer

Lord, give me eyes to see beyond the tragedy of the day to the wonder of eternity. If I cannot see Your purpose, give me the strength to endure with joy. I'm so grateful for all the gifts the You've bestowed on me—help me count my blessings, love my neighbors, and use my energy to pour into others. Amen.

Discussion Questions

1. How does knowing Jesus change our perspective about misfortune?

_____

2. When was a time you focused on truth rather than joy?

_____

3. How is focusing on joy a solution, even when truth is harsh and challenging?

_____

Christmas Commission

Do a little research to discover where the best Christmas light decorations are. Drive there at night and spend some time just basking in their glow.

Day 18

Faithfulness

Let a man so consider us, as servants of Christ and stewards of the mysteries of God. Moreover it is required in stewards that one be found faithful.

1 CORINTHIANS 4:1-2

Benjamin was torn. He really liked this girl he was seeing, but he owed it to his grandmother to pay her a visit in the nursing home. Christmas was coming, after all.

Susan was sweet, smart, and fun. She seemed uncomplicated, something that Benjamin really appreciated. He didn't understand women. Most of them were either silly or manipulative, but Susan behaved quite differently from most girls, he thought. Then again, maybe he misread her. He was afraid to tell her his plan, but time was running out. He rang the bell at her house and waited.

Her little brother Robby answered and stood, with the door open, waiting for Benjamin to speak. This, again. Robby played silly games. After all, the winter cold was wafting into the house, and he didn't seem to care. He enjoyed the power play. He stared at Benjamin. "Yes?"

"I'm picking up your sister."

"Which one?"

"Very funny. I'm here for Susan. She knows I'm coming."

"Sure, she does." Then he turned, shut the door, and Benjamin could hear, "SUSAN!!!" echo through the house and vibrate the glass in the storm door.

Moments later, Susan appeared, looking fresh and happy. "I'll be back later tonight!" she yelled behind her as she closed the door. "Let's go—wait, where are we going?"

"Ah . . . well . . . it's a bit of a surprise, actually."

"I *love* surprises!"

Benjamin laughed uncomfortably as he opened the passenger door for Susan. He got in, started the car, and drove off.

They discussed the end of the semester, the coming holiday, and annoying little brothers on the way, and Benjamin eased the car into a parking spot outside the Waterside Nursing and Care Facility.

"Okay, so, I have an errand to run, and I need to bring you along. And I apologize in advance, okay?"

"Ooh. This sounds serious. What are we talking about?" Susan glanced around, not recognizing the area.

"So, my grandmother is in this nursing home. I have to visit her, but hospitals make me super uncomfortable. I hate them. So, I'm bringing you along for moral support."

"I'm a hostage?" Susan demanded, feigning horror.

"What?! No!"

"Just kidding! Silly! This is no problem at all. I used to be a candy striper. On the cardiac ward. It was fun. Hospitals don't freak me out at all. In fact, I used to pull the electrical wires out of the patients' chests when they were getting ready for discharge or whatever. That was freakin' cool."

"I knew it! I knew you'd be good with this plan!"

"That's why you kept it a secret?"

"Well . . . anyway, let's get this over with."

They walked into the entry, where a large Christmas tree was decorated in mainly red ribbons and large red and silver glass ornaments and asked to find Selma Bixby's room. On their way, Benjamin spotted her, out in the hallway. "There she is," he said to Susan.

The elderly dame was hunched over in her wheelchair, wearing pastel pajamas with a loosely tied light blue robe.

She had a far-away look. Benjamin stood in front of her with his hands in his pockets.

Susan looked from him to Selma and back again. "Well? Aren't you going to introduce me?" she demanded.

"Hi, Gammy. I came to visit you. And I brought my friend, Susan." He gestured awkwardly at Susan.

Susan immediately dropped to her knee, bringing her eye-level with the old woman who was struggling to raise her head, due to her sloped, aged shoulders.

"My name is Susan. I'm in college with Benjamin. We are both studying international relations."

"Oh? How is Benjamin?"

"Well, he's here and can tell you himself."

"I'm fine, Gammy. School is going well." Benjamin was stilted and uncomfortable. He looked around at the quiet nurses' station and the other slowly moving patients in the hallway.

"How about we take you for a little ride, seeing as how you are already in your wheelchair?"

"That would be fine. . . . "

Susan helped Selma place her feet onto the footrests and then began slowly pushing the chair down the hallway. Selma looked around and said, "This is very nice. Thank you."

At the end of the hallway was a small seating area overlooking the parking lot and beyond to some vacant land. Susan maneuvered the chair to give Selma the view, then took a seat in a chair facing her. Benjamin stood behind the chair and said quite loudly, "Are they feeding you enough in here, Gammy? I heard you haven't been feeling well."

Susan stood up and took Benjamin's arm to bring him away. "Listen, please. I'm going to try to make this easier for you. Your grandmother can't look up to take in all six-foot-four of you. She can't turn her head to look at you, so you need to place yourself in her field of vision, please. And she's ill, not deaf, okay? Try to fill her needs, and stop concentrating on how you feel, just for the time we are here, okay?"

Benjamin fixed Susan with an apprehensive gaze, taking in her commanding demeanor. He settled himself, absorbing her advice. "Okay."

"Good. Grab that chair over there and sit here with me, in front of Miss Selma."

They sat there, out of the way of the nursing staff and doctors and visited with Gammy for a full hour before taking her back to her room.

"Thank you for visiting me, Benjamin, and for bringing this delightful young lady."

"Merry Christmas, Miss Selma," wished Susan as they left.

Prayer

Heavenly Father, who holds us all in the palm of His hand, grant me the patience, and fill my heart with Your love so I can reflect Your peace and caring to the world around me. Open my eyes to the needs of others and create in me a steadfast hold on compassion. Amen.

Discussion Questions

1. How does knowing how Christ ministered help us minister to others?

   _____

2. When was the last time you volunteered to help someone, unexpectedly?

   _____

3. How can you be of service to someone, today?

   _____

Christmas Commissions

1. Get some Christmas books from the library! *The Night Before Christmas*, *How the Grinch Stole Christmas*, *The Best Christmas Pageant Ever*, etc. Ask the librarian for suggestions.
2. Pop popcorn to eat while reading aloud and make an old-fashioned popcorn and cranberry garland for the tree.
3. Have a family slumber party beneath or around the tree!

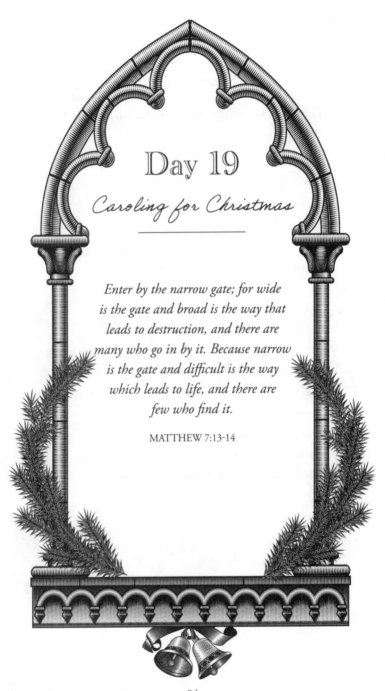

Day 19

Caroling for Christmas

---

*Enter by the narrow gate; for wide
is the gate and broad is the way that
leads to destruction, and there are
many who go in by it. Because narrow
is the gate and difficult is the way
which leads to life, and there are
few who find it.*

MATTHEW 7:13-14

Jenny was an American girl, living in Sweden. She had been there for a few years, working for an American company that had brought her over from the states. With Swedish ancestry, Jenny had been overjoyed at the prospect of moving to her favorite city, and once she landed in England, nothing disappointed her—not even the sometimes-dismal weather, which Jenny found to be cozy and comforting.

Jenny was out wandering the streets, as she loved to do in London, especially around Christmastime, and she stumbled upon a little Christmas carol event happening outside an antique bookstore in a narrow street called Cheswick Chase. The charming, upscale street was lined with elegant antique shops and hung with bright, festive Christmas decorations. Each shop displayed an old-fashioned type of sign from its doorway out into the street, so, looking down the street from Jenny's vantage point, the signs sweetly framed a serene, picturesque scene. Snow had piled up on the storefronts and street curbs but was trampled down enough in the sidewalks as to allow easy passage.

In the festivities in front of the bookstore were professional opera singers, engaged as carolers for the event, and the bookseller who had arranged the affair for the block served free holiday snacks and warm drinks for everyone who stopped by. It was a true holiday celebration with strangers greeting each other and enjoying the outpouring of Christmas cheer to all. The singers had all been singing at various venues all day, with the quaint bookshop as their last stop. After their final round of carols, everyone enjoyed the refreshments and hung around in the street chatting. Jenny, who reveled in the Christmas caroling spirit, caught the distinct impression that the entire occasion was secular, despite its genesis, but no bother. To her, Christmas would always be Christmas, the birth of Jesus and the coming of the Light of the World. There's just something quite seductive about this season that gets people feeling charitable and friendly, she believed.

As the evening reluctantly drew to its end, the attendees were enjoying themselves such that no one seemed to notice the chilly air, the tardiness of the hour and encroaching darkness, or the weathered old homeless man with a crutch under one arm and missing teeth obvious through his grizzled, bushy beard, until he walked into their midst to beg.

The bedraggled but impervious drifter, abruptly in their midst, just as suddenly professed that Jesus was his "best friend" to the bewildered group. A few carolers and audience even raised their eyebrows and some uncomfortable mumbling traded on the crisp air.

Impervious to their gossip, and as though he knew that there were professional singers in the crowd, the guileless fellow decided that he wanted a carol, and he began to sing *Silent Night* in a raspy, quivering voice.

Oh dear, thought Jenny, *perhaps the singers will be annoyed, as they're very tired, and the crowd seems disinclined. I'm so embarrassed for him. . . .*

But no. Quietly, two of the singers began to join in with him (and to be fair, his voice was quite pleasing once he got under way.)

Gradually, the rest of the singers took up the tune, their voices coming from all around, being now scattered from mingling with the crowd. Once committed, they really cut loose, and the touching, uplifting song rang through the air. People, singing or just mouthing the words, felt smiles sneak onto their lips and merriment enveloped the crowd.

"Now," said the homeless man enthusiastically afterwards, "Let's do *O Come All Ye Faithful*! Come on!" Without hesitation, off he launched into the next song and again the singers joined in, gathering around him now, as he sang his heart out, while conducting with one hand.

Then came the grand finale. He said something to one of the singers, who turned to us all and announced, "OK, everyone, we're going to do *Amazing Grace*."

"But first," interjected the delighted and guileless visitor, "I'm going to say grace."

Although this secular crowd seemingly desired nothing of the sort, they were silently respectful as he looked up to Heaven and gave fervent thanks, finishing with "Lord Jesus, this one's for You!"

Then he began to sing *Amazing Grace*, and all joined in, though, as the singers didn't know the second verse, they hummed along in harmony for it, as a kind of background chorus. He sang so fervently his eyes shone bright with tears, bringing others to strong emotions, as well.

"Happy Christmas!" cried the man when he'd done. "I may be homeless, but my faith is like a rock. Happy Christmas!" Beaming, he went around and hugged several of the audience and singers.

The singers even exchanged details with him, as they ran community singing programs, and recognized that he had some ability. A few people happily gave him some cash. (There wasn't much food left by then, unfortunately.)

"Happy Christmas!" he called out to everyone, "And God bless you!"

Satisfied and grinning, he turned and hobbled away down the street, into the enveloping winter night, leaving most of them quietly exhilarated and wondering at the power of an individual lacking in all the things they thought they should hold dear.

Prayer

Lord, show me what to hold dear and what to release to You. Give my life the simplicity it needs to allow me to focus on You. Don't let me be distracted by the earthly desires that others covet. Let me covet You! Amen.

Discussion Questions

1. How could the guy with nothing be so joyful at Christmas?

   _____

2. Why do people focus on material things, instead of on eternity?

   _____

3. How might you help others to experience the eternal love of Jesus today?

   _____

Christmas Commissions

1. Leave cookies in your mailbox for your mailperson to find. Think of other service people whom you should acknowledge for their help during the year and reach out to them with some similar kind of blessing.

2. Arrange a cookie swap with friends—but insist on homemade goodies! Or organize a cookie bake, where you make three different kinds of cookies and enlist your friends' help in mixing and baking together!

Day 20

Heaven

---

*Set your mind on things above, not on
things on the earth. For you died, and
your life is hidden with Christ in God.
When Christ who is our life appears,
then you also will appear
with Him in glory.*

COLOSSIANS 3:2-4

In New Zealand, Christmas comes in the summer. There are no snowball fights, no icicles, and no snowmen on anyone's front lawn. Sam and I would always travel back to the states for the holiday, but for our dog it was a different story. She couldn't go in and out of the country as easily as we humans could because of the island nation's quarantine restrictions, so our neighbors took her for us. They had owned a pug but had lost her the prior year and didn't want the full-time commitment of having a pet, so babysitting for us was their ideal role.

It was still cool this early Christmas morning, though, when Peter opened the door to let Gizmoe, our eight-pound Brussels Griffon with a pushed-in face, out on the back lawn.

"Hurry up, Gizzy! We've got to get our coffee and start the day—it's Christmas and there's a lot to do!" Peter spoke with the soft native Kiwi twang. The lanky, retired gentleman stood on his expansive back porch and watched, although, as the country has no real animal predators and the yard was fully enclosed, safety wasn't a concern.

Takapuna Lake lay at the bottom of Peter's gently sloping yard. Its waters were serene and undisturbed, unmindful that, in another hour, the rowers would be out on the lake and some guy with a bullhorn and an air gun would be blasting instructions for lining up the racing boats so the entire neighborhood would hear.

Gizmoe ran down the lawn, looking for a good spot to relieve herself. As she did, a grey goose landed gracefully on the lawn in front of her. He walked around, gauging his surroundings. He picked at the grass a bit, keeping an eye on the small reddish-brown creature that had started cautiously approaching him.

Peter, still on the deck, descended the stairs softly while he watched the two curious animals guardedly gauge each other. He couldn't believe his eyes. Gizmoe slowly approached the bird, and the large steel-colored goose stretched his neck out to reach her with his beak to get a closer look at her.

Gizmoe decided right then to tempt him into playing with her. She bowed down on her front legs with her little tail in the air, taunting him. She ran in several circles in front of him trying to get him to chase her. At one point, he reared up and back, flapping his wings to display his great size, but then he just fluffed his feathers and settled back down.

Gizzy then walked straight up to him, as if to say, "Well, if you don't want to play, what do you want?"

Peter stood in awestruck silence, though he wished he had already grabbed his coffee. He took a deep breath in and looked around to see that he was the only person in the world seeing this incredible scene.

Gizmoe and the goose touched noses, their forms silhouetted by the glistening lake water behind them. Then the goose flew away and Gizmoe turned and ran to Peter, as if to say, "Didja see that? (Look, Pa! No hands!)"

"Woah, Gizzy! Look what you just did! You made friends with a goose—and that doesn't happen every day! Good girl!"

He brought Giz inside and fed her breakfast (after getting his coffee) while he told his wife the entire story. It seemed so incredible, he half-doubted he had dreamt it up, but the next day the goose came back and was waiting on the lawn for his playdate with the tiny dog.

Gizmoe ran down the lawn to ask him to chase her, but he refused, simply standing in the middle of her zooming across the lawn and around him, then rearing up to flap his wings, as if to say, "Slow down, and come over here for your morning smooch."

Then Gizmoe, again, walked gently up to him and they tenderly touched noses.

The goose visited every day like that for the rest of their holiday, until Gizmoe returned home to us. Peter and his wife felt so blessed to be witnesses to God's wonder in their lives.

Prayer

How righteous is the Glory of the King.
How splendid is His beautiful creation.
I know full-well the greatness of His love for me.
His wondrous works give cause for my elation.
He covers me in grace so lovingly,
And treasures every prayer I send above.
So who am I that He should cherish me?
I am His loving child and, Amen, I'm His love.

Discussion Questions

1. When have you witnessed a small miracle in your life?

   _____

2. How did it change your relationship with God?

   _____

3. Why was God's first job for Adam to name the animals?

   _____

Christmas Commissions

1. Organize a Christmas scavenger hunt for the kids.
2. Sing Christmas karaoke. Put on a real show (with potentially a lot of laughs) by throwing a Christmas karaoke party! There are endless songs you can include, and you can make it a game by telling people they have to skip over certain words, like *Santa*! If they mess up, they're out.

Day 21

Celebrate

———

I say to you that likewise there will be more joy in heaven over one sinner who repents than over ninety-nine just persons who need no repentance.

LUKE 15:7

Savannah sat anxiously by the window, watching for the first car to pull into their newly shoveled driveway. The sun was setting, shining its reddish light into her eyes as she strained to hear car tires on the snow up the street—to no avail. She couldn't stay on the couch, so she moved to the Christmas tree to count gifts again.

Savannah had set the table, folding the napkins into fans and setting them in the water glasses, just like her mother had taught her to do. She was excited that the entire family would soon descend on their house and her mother was buzzing around the kitchen making her preparations. There were so many gifts under the tree, Savannah lost count and had to start over.

Just then, the doorbell rang. The front door opened, ushering in a gust of chill and a few flakes of snow. Gemma, Kyle, and the twins burst through the doorway shouting, "Merry Christmas!" and shaking snowflakes off their coats.

"Merry Christmas," yelled Mama from the kitchen. "C'mon in! You're almost late!"

"You always say that," said Gemma, taking off the twins' coats and then shrugging out of hers.

Kyle addressed the boys, "You kids stay out of trouble and no cookies until after dinner, understood?" Both eleven-year-olds faced him and nodded. "Yes, Papa," they answered in unison.

Just then the door opened again to reveal Gramps, "Hello! Is there still food in this joint? We didn't miss it, did we?"

"Dad!" Mama called from the kitchen. "You know we wouldn't dream of starting without you!" Graham came through the door behind him and headed, casserole in hand, straight to the kitchen.

Right after her came Joey, tall, dark, and charming. He immediately picked up Savannah and twirled her around, making her dizzy, and her stomach leap. He drew her in for a hug while she snuck her scrawny arms around his neck as tightly as she could.

"Dang, girl, you're getting soooo big! What did you wish for, for Christmas?"

"I asked for a pony. I just love horses!"

"Horses, huh? Why didn't anyone tell me?" he said, loud enough for Mama, his sister, to hear in the kitchen."

Mama laughed and answered, "You wouldn't dare, Joey."

Soon the entire family was seated around the table, praying over their meal. They thanked God for His blessings and the goodness of the holiday that celebrated the greatest gift mankind ever had known. Then they all dug in and ate to their hearts' content, and more.

After dinner, most helped clear the table while Gramps prepared to read from the Bible for the whole clan. Because there were so many adults in the kitchen, the kids were sent off the play in the living room, by the tree, while Gramps stoked the fire by the cozy recliner.

The boys were comparing Christmas dinner bellies. *Gross*, thought Savannah as she started counting the gifts again. That's when she noticed the tiny box in the shiny red wrapping paper behind a larger, colorfully wrapped package. This little rouge cube sported a bright silver poof, like nothing she'd seen before. It was like someone had tied together a bunch of tree foil into a pom-pom. There was a notecard attached by a silver cord under the poof that read, "To Savannah. From Jesus' friend."

"What in the . . . " Savannah said softly to herself. Her mind raced to figure out who was giving her the gift and what it might be.

She could hardly sit still during the reading, and even less while each took turns opening their gifts. It was fun to see what other people received, but each time she opened a gift—and they were wonderful—she contemplated what was inside the little red box.

Finally, Joey brought her the box to open. "Oh, Joey, what did you get her?" asked Mama. He always found something that excited and pleased Savannah, so she was thrilled to know it came from him. "Open it," he encouraged her.

She carefully removed the poof from the top. "That's an interesting bow," said Gramps. Then she peeled the tape from the facing paper, while the twins grumbled that it always took Savannah too long to open a gift!

Inside the box was a small silver charm, like for a charm bracelet, but this one was on a beautiful silver chain. It was a horse with a saddle, rearing, just like in the westerns that she loved to watch. Also inside the box was a folded paper, which she unfolded:

This certificate entitles the bearer
to ten riding lessons at the QR ranch.

Savannah looked at her mom, then at Joe, then her face screwed up, and then she burst into tears. Joey was confused. "What? You don't like it? I figured you'd love it!"

Savannah nodded, choking on her joy. "It's the most wonderful present in the entire world!" She ran and grabbed his face and smooched him right on the cheek.

"Joey, how do you always do that? Find just the right thing?"

Joey shrugged. Gramps said, "It's because he listens. He's always had that attention to detail. It's a gift!"

Prayer

Heavenly Lord of Hosts, please make me receptive to hearing the hearts of those around me. Give me patience to listen to the small unspoken thoughts as well as the loud ones. Let me peek into the desires of my loved ones and even those I don't know, so I may provide the vehicle for Your purposes. Amen.

Discussion Questions

1. Why does the lost sheep excite so much attention when it is found?

2. How are we often like the lost sheep?

3. What is the easiest hack for choosing gifts for others?

Christmas Commissions

1. Read the Christmas story from Luke 2:1-20 in the Bible out loud.
2. Find and shop at a holiday market.

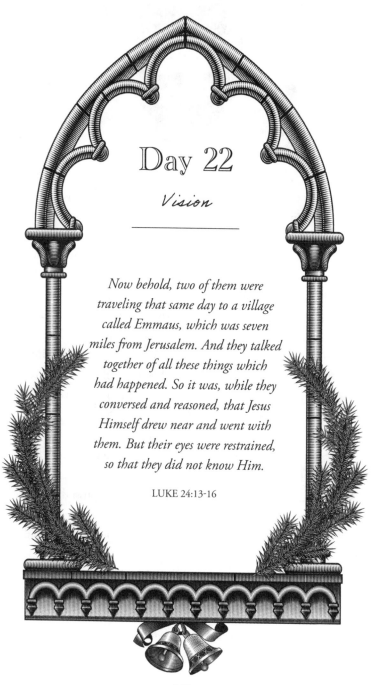

Day 22

Vision

Now behold, two of them were traveling that same day to a village called Emmaus, which was seven miles from Jerusalem. And they talked together of all these things which had happened. So it was, while they conversed and reasoned, that Jesus Himself drew near and went with them. But their eyes were restrained, so that they did not know Him.

LUKE 24:13-16

Bobby felt invisible. He had worked at the big box store for almost a year already, and he figured he was due for a promotion soon, but it was like his bosses could never see how hard he worked. He always showed up on time and often stayed later than expected, just to get the task he'd been given done.

It's true, he wasn't very talkative with his coworkers. They were all substantially older than he. He had nothing really to say to them, but neither was he ever rude or off-putting. He kept his head down and did the job. He served the customers as best he could, when he was on the floor. Mostly, he worked on inventory, which he enjoyed. He liked things to be orderly. The job was always his focus. But a little extra cash would be nice for the coming holiday, so, when could he expect to get that promotion?

It was a still, frosty morning when Bobby pulled up to his parking space at the back of the store. He punched in and put his lunch in the break room. He was about to open the door when he heard voices outside. Not wanting to push the door into them, he waited for them to pass by.

". . . then you'd have to let someone on your floor go. Did you have someone in mind?"

"I do, in fact. The young guy, Bobby. Most of the others are happy where they are, but I could stand to lose him."

Bobby cringed. It was the worst possible news, and just before Christmas! He knew he shouldn't be listening in on other's conversations. He quickly reached out and pulled a chair back to let it fall, making a loud noise.

The door opened.

Mack, Bobby's boss, stood in the doorway. "Everything okay in here?"

"Sorry, sir, I guess I got up too quickly and knocked my chair over. No harm done, though," he continued, righting the chair.

Mack checked his watch as two more employees entered the break room behind him. "Well, you're right on time. Let's all have a good day on the floor today."

"Yes, sir," Bobby answered.

"And Bobby, come see me at the end of your shift, please."

"Yes, sir."

Mack seemed so cavalier about firing me, thought Bobby angrily.

The day went by in a blur. Bobby was despondent, but he tried to keep his wits about him. He thought of other places he could apply to work. He wondered whether he should even ask for a reference from his boss. He wondered how easy it would be to find another job during the holidays. There were usually seasonal hires, but it was already well into the season, so perhaps it was too late. He thought, *and here, I was thinking I might be due for a promotion! I'm such an idiot!*

He considered arguments against being let go, dejectedly realizing it was probably futile. He pondered retaliating— they never realized how hard he worked, anyway, so, maybe sabotage would show them—while acknowledging he lacked the requisite spite to do anything. He couldn't live with himself if he did, anyway.

113

Instead, he reasoned that if he could put in his best day ever, he could exit with his head held high. They just didn't realize they were letting their best employee go, and that's obviously because of bad management.

All these things raced through Bobby's head as he worked, and soon he was just busy getting his job done, as he always had. Towards the end of the day, though, dread set in again. He didn't want to go into Mack's office. He didn't want to hear those words. He felt like the sword of Damocles hung over his head.

At 6:05 p.m., he punched out and slowly walked to Mack's office. He saw Mack though the glass door, reading at his desk. Bobby knocked and waited.

Mack looked up, and his face showed consternation. He waved Bobby in with a concerning gesture of impatience.

"Bobby. It's good to see you. I just got some bad news. . . ."

Interrupting, the words spilled out of Bobby so quickly, Mack was surprised into silence. "Sir, I'm always on time and I do good work. No one has ever criticized my efforts, that I know of. And I'm dedicated. And I can improve, if you tell me how." Bobby paused.

"I'm glad to hear it."

"Then why are you firing me?"

"At Christmas? Ridiculous! My plan was to promote you! We are installing a new inventory system and I need someone to learn the software and help smooth the transition. I know from your resume that you have computer skills, and you already know the operations part, so I wanted to offer you the job. Why on earth did you think you were being fired?"

Bobby felt shame. He couldn't confess he had accidentally eavesdropped, but what could he possibly say? "I . . . I guess, well, you've never called me into your office before. . . ."

"If you want the job, it comes with a raise, of course."

"I do, sir. Thank you!"

"Great! You'll start training next week. Merry Christmas, Bobby."

"Thank you! Uh, Sir? You seemed so angry when I came in . . . ?"

"Ah, don't remind me. My favorite football player was just suspended! It's a disaster."

Bobby laughed with Mack, realizing Mack's harsh look resulted only from his love of sports.

Prayer

Dad up in the sky, please help keep my feet on the ground. Bring me closer to appreciation and further from misinterpretations and silly conclusions. Give me patience to wait for revelations as they come, and understanding when they do. And thanks for the patience and understanding You give me every day. Amen.

Discussion Questions

1. Why do you suppose Jesus kept those men from recognizing him?

   _____

2. Have you ever made a wrong assumption and regretted it?

   _____

3. What might be some wrong assumptions you're harboring about God?

   _____

Christmas Commissions

1. Do a family game night. Play card games as a group, charades, or a board game like Settlers of Catan. See other game suggestions at SorboStudios.com.
2. Make hot cocoa, light a fire in the fireplace (or on the TV!), snuggle up, and read a Christmas story or book out loud as a family.

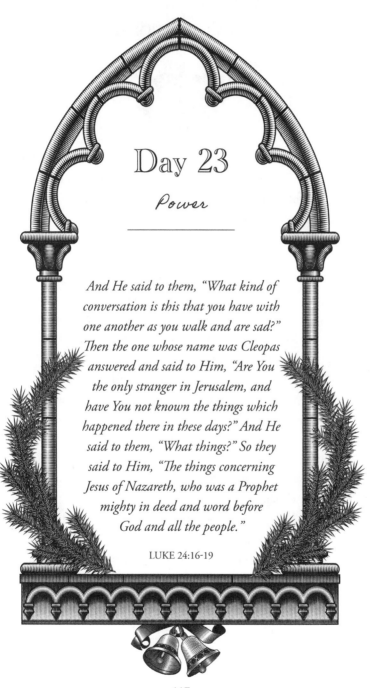

Day 23

Power

---

*And He said to them, "What kind of
conversation is this that you have with
one another as you walk and are sad?"
Then the one whose name was Cleopas
answered and said to Him, "Are You
the only stranger in Jerusalem, and
have You not known the things which
happened there in these days?" And He
said to them, "What things?" So they
said to Him, "The things concerning
Jesus of Nazareth, who was a Prophet
mighty in deed and word before
God and all the people."*

LUKE 24:16-19

Standing in line to board the plane, Travis went over in his head the bullet points for his new client, whom he would see the following morning. The line moved slowly, and Travis shifted anxiously as he waited to pass the smiling flight attendant and get to his seat.

He moved down the aisle. *Twenty-one C,* he thought, watching row numbers as he passed by them. He planned to review the entire presentation on the short flight out to Austin. He stopped in front of an empty seat, next to a lanky young bald man who sat with an unmistakable look of concern on his face. Travis felt a distinctive heaviness on the in the air.

"Mind if I join you?" Travis asked light-heartedly.

The young man pulled out an ear bud, questioning.

"Oh. I was just saying 'Hi,'" said Travis, heaving his overnight roller bag over head and easing into the seat. "You heading home?"

His seatmate shook his head. "Not yet. I'm heading to a funeral, actually."

"Oh, I'm so sorry! My condolences. And at Christmas, no less."

"Well, conveniently, I was going to be traveling home for the holiday, anyway. So, it's just an extra stop. But this certainly puts a damper on the whole journey."

The young man began to replace his ear bud but was stopped by Travis asking, "Were you very close to the deceased? Family?"

"Yeah, my mother's brother. He was a great uncle. Just a great guy. We're not sure what happened, but they suspect he had a stroke. Mom's pretty upset about it. He wasn't that old, you know?"

"Why suspect stroke? Did he have high blood pressure?"

The young man nodded. "Yeah, and he was on heart meds, too. At least he went fast, and they say he wouldn't even have known what hit him. He's always had trouble with his heart, medically speaking. As a human, his heart worked perfectly."

Travis didn't understand. He looked quizzically at him. "He loved people. Absolutely. Went to church twice a week, helped, was very involved. He loved me, too. I was named after him. We used to play a lot when I was a boy. Wrestle with my brother. He always had time for me. Always. Birthday cards every year. Christmas every time he could get out to us. I made a habit of calling him every weekend, just to check in. Man, I'm gonna miss him."

"Sounds like he was a good guy. I'm sorry for your loss. I had a favorite uncle. He passed about six years ago. He even lived with us for a bit, while I was growing up."

They sat in silence while the flight attendants made their announcements, and the plane began to taxi to the runway.

The young man sighed. "It's gonna be a sad Christmas this year."

"Does it have to be?"

"What do you mean?"

"Well, uhm, where is he, now? I mean, he was a professing Christian, right?"

"Yeah, he was. I'm not, though."

"Well, that may be a conversation for another time, but rest assured, even though you don't believe in heaven, that's where he is. And that's why he loved everyone, like you say. He was showing the world the love of Christ. That's a bold testimony."

"I suppose. I just wish I had more assurance, you know. I get that folks believe, but people believe anything these days. How do you know?"

Travis only took a moment to answer. "That's easy. You must look. Research. Read the Bible and watch some apologists, like John Lennox. He's a famous mathematician and an amazing speaker. If you really want to know, you will find the truth"

"John Lennox?" The young man made a note of the name on his phone.

"Most people say they want to know but they refuse to sacrifice their pride, which keeps them from knowing. You seem smarter than that. And by the way, you don't have to believe in heaven to know that's where he is. He believed—and that's enough."

The young man regarded Travis for a moment.

"You make it sound so simple."

Travis laughed. "Because it is simple! There's no reason to complicate things!"

The young man nodded, trying to understand. "My Uncle Travis used to say that. 'Let's not complicate things, Travis.'" The young man used a lower register to imitate his favorite uncle.

Travis looked at him, astonished. "*My* name is Travis."

"That's . . . weird."

"Yeah. Funny." Travis took out his computer so he could work some more on his presentation. Then he turned to the younger Travis. "Travis, is there a way you can grieve for the loss of your favorite uncle from your day-to-day life, but celebrate his arrival in heaven?"

The young man looked at Travis and smiled softly. "That's a great idea," he said quietly. "He would like that, I'm sure. I'll talk to my mom about it. Thanks."

Prayer

I pray for truth, wisdom, discernment, and understanding. I pray that those who don't know Jesus would meet Him today, and that He would supernaturally enter their hearts and minds, blessing them with His enduring love. Amen.

Discussion Questions

1. Why do you think Cleopas seemed disappointed that the stranger in the verse above didn't know of Jesus?

2. What consolation does Travis give young Travis over the death of his favorite uncle?

3. How might you testify to an unbeliever today?

Christmas Commission

Make a gingerbread house, using a kit or baking, and piecing it together. Use icing, candy decorations, and even add some store-bought cookies to make a gorgeous Christmas scene!

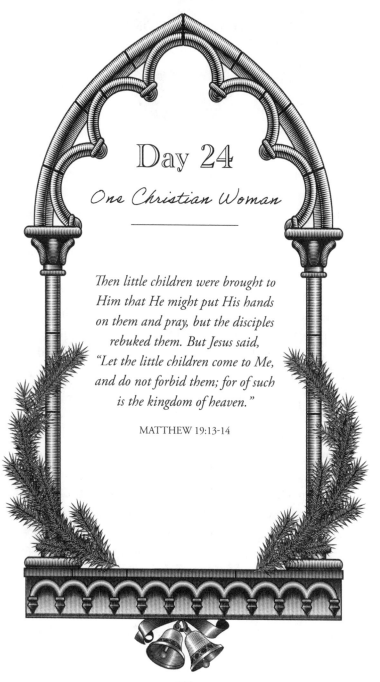

Day 24

One Christian Woman

Then little children were brought to Him that He might put His hands on them and pray, but the disciples rebuked them. But Jesus said, "Let the little children come to Me, and do not forbid them; for of such is the kingdom of heaven."

MATTHEW 19:13-14

123

Winston Churchill's parents were not the doting adults you might imagine producing such a valiant freedom fighter. In fact, they were terribly, astonishingly cold to little Winston. Randolf and Jennie Churchill were social climbers of the highest magnitude, sacrificing all semblance of family life for their societal ambitions. They sent young Churchill off to boarding schools and ignored his long letters and plaintive requests for visits from them. In fact, when his father did a speaking engagement next door to Churchill's school, he didn't even stop by to see his child. It seemed to be his opinion that young Churchill was retarded, even, to the point that he disdained his offspring, often raging at him, and comparing him unfavorably to his younger sibling.

Providentially, shortly after young Winston was born, his parents hired a nanny for him in the person of Mrs. Elizabeth Anne Everest. She was the truest expression of the traditional nanny: plump, joyful, loving, and formidably protective of Winston. He called her "Woom," and she quickly became the center of his world, while his distracted parents couldn't care less. In short, he adored and revered her.

Although young Churchill was a solitary child and often away at boarding school, Mrs. Everest was his rock—his comforter, confidant, and counsel. She provided for him a touchstone and sounding board, and her strong Christian faith and sincere convictions informed their entire relationship. She bestowed on Churchill her fervent beliefs and trained him in passionate prayer. Together, they studied the Bible and she taught him to memorize scriptures. She also helped him understand the world through a distinctly and unapologetically Christian lens.

Winston was not a gifted student and nearly flunked out of school as a young child. Later, when he attended a different school that was more militarily and pragmatically focused, he began to excel, proving to himself and others that when given interesting things to learn, he could apply himself. It wasn't, however, until he joined the military and turned twenty that he began to learn in earnest, driven by his own desire and need to know.

Personally, I am always ready to learn,
although I do not always like being taught.

WINSTON CHURCHILL

In his adult years, when he found himself under fire on foreign battlefields or in the most grueling political challenges, it was the earnest prayers Mrs. Everest had diligently taught him that he prayed.

The most important quality that Churchill possessed, if we could choose one, would likely be his unwavering faith in the good, the true, and the beautiful. It was his Christian conviction that made him brave beyond measure and wise beyond his years.

Shortly after the Pearl Harbor attack, Churchill traveled with his ministers to pay a visit to President Franklin D. Roosevelt. On Christmas Eve of that year, Churchill broadcast to the world from the White House on the twentieth annual observation of the lighting of the community Christmas tree.

I spend this anniversary and festival far from my country, far from my family, yet I cannot truthfully say that I feel far from home . . . Ill would it be for us this Christmastide if we were not sure that no greed for the land or wealth of any other people, no vulgar ambition, no morbid lust for material gain at the expense of others, had led us to the field. . . . Here, in the midst of war, raging and roaring over all the lands and seas, creeping nearer to our hearts and homes, here, amid all the tumult, we have tonight the peace of the spirit in each cottage home and in every generous heart. Therefore we may cast aside for this night at least the cares and dangers which beset us, and make for the children an evening of happiness in a world of storm. . . . Let us grown-ups share to the full in their unstinted pleasures before we turn again to the stern task and the formidable years that lie before us, resolved that, by our sacrifice and daring, these same children shall not be robbed of their inheritance or denied their right to live in a free and decent world.

And so, in God's mercy, a happy Christmas to you all.

With deep conviction he led England and forces for freedom worldwide to victory over tyranny that sought world-domination. So it must be that we give thanks for Nanny Everest, "Woom," the woman who showed him God's love, and created in him a yearning to be true to, and have abiding faith in, the heavenly Father of us all, the author of our freedom.

Prayer

Lord, we give thanks for those who came before us and for the freedom that Your work on Earth bestowed us. Thank You for your servants and your earthly saints. Let us follow in their footsteps. Amen.

Discussion Questions

1. Why does Jesus tell His disciples that the kingdom of heaven belongs to "such as these"?

2. Why was it important for young Winston to have a nanny who loved him and showed him her faith?

3. How can we encourage others with our own faith?

Christmas Commissions

1. Print out and make some of the free paper toys and decorations here: https://www.thetoymaker.com/Holidays/Christmas/Christmas.html
2. Make cinnamon rolls or a relevant or significant treat from your cultural heritage.

Day 25

Blessing Others

---

*Let nothing be done through selfish
ambition or conceit, but in lowliness
of mind let each esteem others
better than himself.*

PHILIPPIANS 2:3

Sophia used to be a grinch. A verifiable, honest-to-God grinch. She really disliked the holiday. Raised Christian, Sophia had, like so many others, fallen away from the faith—she was a party girl, seeking hedonistic pleasures, as she learned to do from the culture that surrounded her. Don't get this wrong—Sophia had been a good kid at home, but once she left for college, all bets were off. She enjoyed her life and had fun.

Every year, when Christmas rolled around, while Sophia celebrated the time off with friends, there was a weight to her happiness. She sent gifts home but resented the judgment she felt she received from that end, and so, she begrudged buying the gifts she sent. She eventually came to feel that the holiday was more like a celebration of her failure as a person—to live up to expectations or perform as the dutiful Christian she was supposedly raised to be.

The problem stemmed from the family's lack of true Christian faith. Sure, they went to church, but during the week, it was like they were different people. The TV they watched, the games they played, the ways they behaved, day to day. No wonder her Christian faith didn't "stick." It had never been *real* to Sophia.

Added on top of that, the oppressive necessity of buying gifts for everyone—and the stress of deciding where to draw the line—took a toll on her, too. She *hated* Christmas shopping, the endless and heartless commercialization of the holiday and the cost was no picnic, either. Although she'd be the

129

first to admit she wasn't even a "believing" Christian, to her, it just felt wrong and almost abusive. She felt used, degraded, miserly, and resentful.

One year, Sophia confided her distress about the holiday to her new Christian friend, Janice. "It's awful: the pressure, the expense, the judgment! I just wish I could ignore it and it would just go away! That would make me happy!"

Janice pondered this. Christmas was her very favorite time of year! She wished she could celebrate Christmas for sixty days, instead of twelve! What could she possibly do, she wondered.

Janice asked Sophia where her favorite place in the world was. Sophia said, "The Eiffel Tower. I went there on a school trip and it's where I fell in love with French. I used to hang out there on my breaks as much as I could when I studied in Paris over the summer a few years later. If I could move to France, I'd live right there!"

A week later Janice brought Sophia a gift, wrapped in shiny red foil with a fluffy green bow on top. "It's an early Christmas gift," she explained.

Sophia refused it gently but with embarrassment. "What? Why . . . Didn't we agree to no gifts?"

"I only said that because I knew they made you uncomfortable. But I found this and couldn't resist. Now, don't think it was any great expense or search. It's a little thing, but I wanted you to have it, please."

Sophia reluctantly accepted the gift, but secretly she was pleased. Presents are nice to get, after all.

It was a small music box that played *La Vie En Rose*. It had an image of the Eiffel Tower on it!

Sophia smiled, big, and quietly hugged Janice, who whispered that it made her sad that her friend *hated* Christmas. "I hope that the music will bring you joy to replace your Christmas funk. The gift-giving at Christmas represents the gift the God gave the world, His Son."

Sophia listened to that tune repeatedly that year. Every time she opened the box, she smiled inside. And she thought about Christ.

The next year, Sophia decided she had had enough of feeling overwhelmed. She determined to enjoy the gift-buying she needed to do and release the extra stuff she really didn't need to do, with no apologies. She discovered the freedom to enjoy herself while shopping and thinking of those she cared for and the reason they were important enough to warrant a gift. She even asked Janice to bring her to church and began to discover the reason behind the celebration of Christmas.

That was her best Christmas ever! It was the beginning of Sophia's Christian journey. She replaced the disdain and antipathy with love—even for the humans who over-commercialize the celebration of His birth. "Forgive them, Father, for they know not what they do," became her mantra (after all, it used to be her!) And it all started with a heartfelt gift to a real-live grinch.

Prayer

Jesus asked for forgiveness, even for His mortal enemies. Father, let me ask for forgiveness for my enemies, and the strength of will to forgive them myself. Let me reflect on the Light of the World and the Reason for the Season and honor Him with my attitude towards even those who seek to harm me. Let there be peace on earth, oh God. Amen.

Discussion Questions

1. In what ways did Jesus exemplify servanthood?

2. Why is humility important in serving others?

3. How can we apply the same gentle tactics Janice used to open other non-Christians' hearts to the joys of Christ?

Christmas Commissions

1. Make eggnog. Hold an eggnog tasting.
2. Watch a Christmas movie!
3. Buy or make someone an unexpected, no-strings-attached, gift. Maybe even contrive to give it to them anonymously.

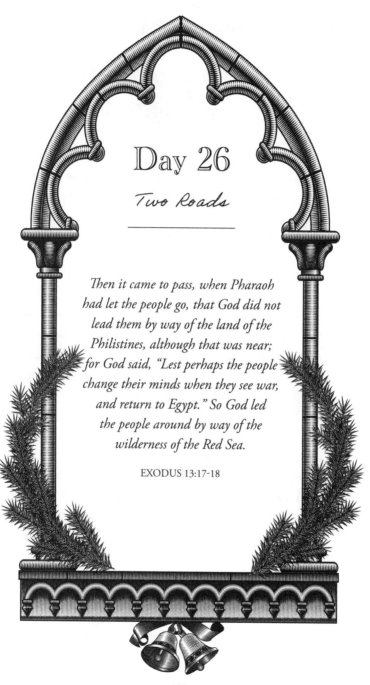

Day 26

Two Roads

---

*Then it came to pass, when Pharaoh
had let the people go, that God did not
lead them by way of the land of the
Philistines, although that was near;
for God said, "Lest perhaps the people
change their minds when they see war,
and return to Egypt." So God led
the people around by way of the
wilderness of the Red Sea.*

EXODUS 13:17-18

Shortly after Kevin turned eleven, his family of seven was happily and excitedly planning a big Christmas trip to Arizona to see the Grand Canyon and ride horses, something he was particularly excited about. Not only was it to be their first trip out of the Minnesota winter, but Kevin loved horses, riding, and westerns! He planned to turn into a verifiable cowboy on this trip, and he was over-the-moon at the prospect.

As "the most wonderful time of the year" approached, both of Kevin's youngest and oldest brothers came down with the flu. They were miserable with the wheezing, coughing, running nose and runnier eyes. Of course, they didn't keep their wretchedness to themselves, and soon the entire family, except Kevin, was sick and in bed. He couldn't believe it; even his mother put herself in bed! And his father, who always seemed the very pillar of health, toppled like a tall redwood, his cough making the entire house shudder.

Kevin was devastated at the prospect of losing what he'd been planning for ages. He made his mother tea and fetched cold compresses for his father. It was all to no avail. . . .

Dad finally made the call: The family vacation to Arizona was canceled!

Disappointed doesn't adequately describe young Kevin's emotions at the time. Add in *frustrated, angry, depressed,* and *lonely.*

He wasn't sick, after all. He felt like the entire family was acting against him. In his eleven-year-old brain, he took this hardship, well, *hard*. He'd been anticipating their great family adventure for a good few months, bragged to everyone about where they were going and what they were going to see, and built it up in his head. The cancellation deflated him. Once Dad wheezed those horrible, devastating words, Kevin stalked out of the house, agonizing.

In fact, he spent as much time outside the house as he could, but the Minnesota winter was biting cold! He visited some non-traveling friends' houses and even took himself to the library one day, just to get out of the cold and away from his traitorous family. The betrayal he felt was profound and, although he was certainly being selfish, their illness had seemingly ruined his entire Christmas!

But one should never judge the story at the middle, because one never seldom sees the silver lining until the end of the story!

That year, after Christmas, during all the post-Christmas sales, Dad, recovered from his influenza battle, took his hard-earned teacher's salary vacation savings and bought for the family their very first color TV and a wonderful home stereo!

The television and the stereo were a kind of luxury their little house had never known. The technology brought them all entertainment that had been long desired but seldom achieved. For years, the stereo played favorite albums and accompanied the children as they grew, filling their growing years with music. The television, too, of course, brought them favorite TV shows and fond family memories watching, every year, *A Charlie Brown Christmas,* which is one of the loveliest presentations of the Gospel message the medium has ever offered.

It didn't take little Kevin long to begin to appreciate the blessings those purchases would become, turning his heart-felt disappointment into an abiding appreciation. Those two Christmas gifts returned dividends for years that could never be rivaled by the family's forfeited trip to the Arizona desert.

Prayer

I pray for patience to understand that the middle of the story is never the end, and that God seeks to prosper and not to punish. God, please let me glimpse beyond my hardships to the greatness of your goodness and give me Your long-suffering heart to abide when I cannot. Amen.

Discussion Questions

1. Why did God protect the freed captives from war when they escaped into the desert?

2. Why should we focus on the big picture, especially in times of distress?

3. How can we help others gain a bigger understanding of God's goodness and workings in their daily lives?

Christmas Commissions

1. Preprint the lyrics for Christmas hymns. Light candles and sing some.
2. Make lefse, a traditional Norwegian potato-dough crêpe that can be filled with butter and brown sugar, Nutella, or jam that Kevin grew up with.

Recipe

In a large pot of salted water, boil 5 pounds of washed/cleaned potatoes. Russets, with their high starch/low moisture content, work well. Cook until soft, drain, cool, peel, and dice. Remove any hardened bits and rice potatoes (with a ricer) while still warm. Melt 1 stick of butter and stir into the riced potatoes. Pat this mixture into a 9" × 13" pan and let cool uncovered. Refrigerate overnight, uncovered (to dry out more).

If you are using a mixer, work in batches. For every 4 cups potato mixture, use:

1.5 cups flour
1 teaspoon salt
2 teaspoons sugar
0.5 cups heavy cream

Blend the riced potatoes, sugar, flour, salt, and heavy cream until well-integrated. Roll the dough into golf ball sized balls and press gently between your palms. The size depends on what you are using for a griddle. Too big won't fit a stove-top pan, but the standard lefse griddle is quite large and can accept much more dough at a time. Place flattened dough balls back into the 9" × 13" pan and refrigerate, so the dough stays cold. Preheat your griddle or skillet surface to 400°–450°, depending on your speed. Sprinkle the rolling pin and surface generously with flour.

Remove a couple of patties from the fridge at a time so they stay cool. Sprinkle flour on each patty before rolling. Roll out until thin. Using a lefse stick (a long, narrow specialized spatula), gently slide it under the rolled pastry, back and forth, to detach it from the surface. If not fully detached, it will tear. With the lefse stick in the center of the sheet, gently lift the crêpe off the board and transfer to your heated surface. Cook for about 45 seconds until the lefse has some light-brown spots, then flip. Grill another 30–45 seconds. Finished lefse are pale with small light-brown spots.

Let each sheet cool thoroughly before stacking, to discourage any moisture from collecting between the sheets. Enjoy with butter and brown sugar, or any other way your heart desires!

Day 27

Slow to Believe

---

*The He said to them, O foolish ones,
and slow of heart to believe in
all that the prophets have spoken!
Ought not the Christ to have suffered
these things and to enter into His
glory?" And beginning at Moses and
all the Prophets, He expounded to
them in all the Scriptures the things
concerning Himself.*

LUKE 24: 25-27

139

Tanya's face was red. She felt like bursting into tears, but her pride wouldn't let her.

"Well?" Randy asked. He was visibly infuriated and with good reason. He had come home early from a work trip that should have been several more days, but the job site hadn't been prepared properly and would require at least another week's work before he could get in there to finish. The boss decided they'd be better served just planning on coming back after the holiday. While it was a nice reprieve, it messed up Randy's after-holiday plans, so the schedule change wasn't the boon his boss might have imagined.

Still fuming over the unexpected postponement, as he walked up the drive to the front door, he'd noticed the huge dent in the front bumper of his brand-new silver truck! Luckily, his daughter was home and came running when he summoned her for an explanation.

Tanya was torn. If she were to admit that she had put the dent in his truck, he might never let her drive it again. But it wasn't really her fault, anyway. She wanted desperately to be anywhere but facing him outside in the cold winter air. Snowflakes descended softly and silently, as Tanya envisioned diamond-hard icicles forming inside her father's heart.

He loved that truck. He had saved for it, negotiated the deal for his trade-in, and was so excited to bring it back home last week. It was her first time driving it, and the unthinkable had happened!

"It wasn't my fault," she whispered.

He seemed to get even angrier, if that was possible. "*What*?!"

"Can I please explain, Daddy?"

"You took my brand-new truck without asking me and got in an accident. What more is there for me to know?"

She couldn't answer. How was she to explain, to avoid his ire? *The only way around it is through,* she told herself. Then, in the next beat, she thought, *What a stupid saying. . . .*

"You borrowed my truck when I was out of town. You didn't even get my permission. Then, you didn't tell me it was damaged! How irresponsible are you, actually?"

"I'm not, Daddy! Listen, the accident wasn't my fault, actually."

He interrupted, "I'm supposed to believe that?"

"Daddy, please let me finish!" she pleaded. "I only borrowed it because Mom said it would be okay with you. I'm not blaming Mom, but I couldn't reach you and she said it would be okay."

"All right, I'm listening. . . . "

"I had committed to going and I couldn't really let my friends down—Stacy was counting on me to be there for her December graduation and there weren't going to be that many people, so if I didn't go, she'd know it."

"Fair enough. How did you get in the accident?"

"It's so dumb, really. I was parallel parked and the gal parking in front of me just slammed her gas pedal, hitting us while we were still in the truck! Like she didn't even know we were there. It was a jolt, I tell you, because she was driving a big car, herself.

"I hopped out to inspect the damage, and so did she. I got her number and she promised to cover the damages but asked me not to call her insurance company. Apparently, her husband owns a body shop, so she can get it handled this week. I was going to take care of it so you wouldn't even know about it. I even have photos of everything. I called the shop, and they are expecting the truck on Monday, and they have a loaner car for me—uh—us—uh—I mean, you. She is a nice lady, but she told me she had just put down her dog who was 15 years old. She had tears in her eyes. I felt really bad for her, Daddy."

Randy was convicted. It was his turn for the red face and heat beneath his skin. He understood he had no reason to take out his work frustration on his daughter, regardless of the state of his truck. The accident wasn't her fault, and he had jumped to some nasty conclusions that were unwarranted. He would have to apologize, and fast, but that was the hard part. It's never fun to admit when you're wrong.

The only way around it is through. How many had he told Tanya that? Too many to count, and now it applied to him. He took a deep breath.

"Tanya, I'm sorry. I acted harshly. In my defense, I'm perturbed about my work, and coming home early to discover this. . . . "

"It's okay, Daddy. I'd be upset, too. I was hoping to get it repaired before you ever found out, 'cause it's only superficial. But you have reason to be upset."

"Not at you, though. I apologize and I'll try to avoid jumping to conclusions again in the future."

"Thanks, Dad. I'm sorry, too."

Prayer

Jesus, sometimes I'm so wrong. It's so difficult to apologize to even those I love. Give me the strength of character, please, to ask for forgiveness of others, even as I ask it of You for my transgressions. Guide me from my hubris to humility. Help me to act more humbly and judge less harshly. Amen.

Discussion Questions

1. What does Jesus do after He rebukes the doubters in the scripture passage above?

2. When was your embarrassing apology needed?

3. How can Jesus help us gain more humility?

Christmas Commission

Go caroling in your neighborhood as a family or a group of people. Print out the carols for people to follow along more easily with the words. Invite others to join in. If necessary, use your smartphone to play the carols to sing along to.

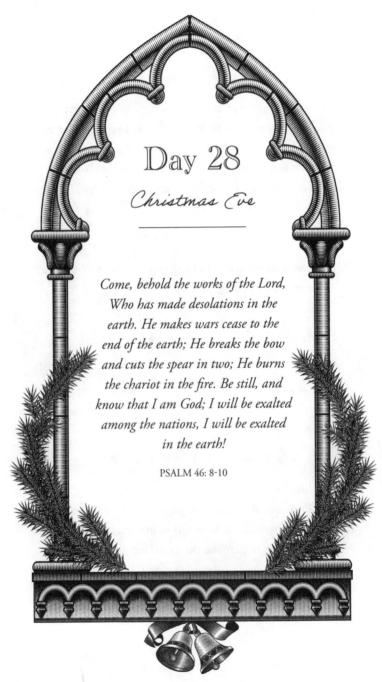

Day 28

Christmas Eve

---

*Come, behold the works of the Lord,
Who has made desolations in the
earth. He makes wars cease to the
end of the earth; He breaks the bow
and cuts the spear in two; He burns
the chariot in the fire. Be still, and
know that I am God; I will be exalted
among the nations, I will be exalted
in the earth!*

PSALM 46: 8-10

The cold in the trenches was barely tempered by the small fires that heated the coffee. Men bundled in sharp woolen coats and lovingly hand-knit scarves shivered as they smoked, the burning tobacco vapors warming their throats and coating their lungs. Most of them never guessed the war would endure longer than a few months—certainly not through the Christmas holiday. Europeans generally agreed that a war of this kind should be quick and virtually painless. The populace reasoned that with their intense self-examination and the advances of the science of the Enlightenment, plus the technological leaps made in warfare, the fighting would be over speedily, and life would resume much as it had before, peacefully, reasonably, and somewhat improved by the elimination of some bad influences.

They couldn't foresee the incredible brutality that their newly developed technology would inflict on everyone involved, the undeniable horrors of the "war to end all wars." (That was, initially, the slogan, meant to inspire confidence, as they entered the war. H.G. Wells, the sci-fi writer believed that defeat of the German military machine would produce a lasting world peace, but we all know how that turned out.)

A consolation to the fighting boys in the trenches was that the winter weather affected all, indiscriminately, so the men fighting on either side were equally miserable. There were tremendous rain showers, sometimes filling the trenches with freezing mud that needed to be shoveled out.

To keep some semblance of normality in this very abnormal war, they sang Christmas carols as the holiday approached. The French sang *Il Est Né (He is Born)*, the Germans sang *O Tannenbaum (Oh Christmas Tree)*, and the English-speakers sang *The First Noel*.

From either side, soldiers would shout across "no man's land" (the terrain between the adversaries' trenches, sometimes no wider than thirty yards) at the other side, sometimes rude remarks and insults, but often just joking comments.

As Christmas drew near, many of the Germans put up Christmas trees, standing them at the tops of the trenches to keep the trench ways clear, but also so the other side could glimpse them. This fomented a sense of camaraderie between the warring sides that both celebrated the birth of Christ. The irony was thick, but orders were orders.

At one point on Christmas Eve, a voice rang out from the German side: "Tomorrow, you no shoot, we no shoot!" The next day was Christmas Day.

The following morning, the day was dismal and gray, but at least there was no rain. Surprising perhaps everyone, five Germans soldiers emerged boldly from their trench, holding up cigarette packets and bottles of champagne. The boys on the French side looked at each other, cautiously wondering what the appropriate response might be. *Could they be serious? No fighting for a day?*

One young man who was disgusted by the war and all its destruction, grabbed the chance for a reprieve and left the trench, standing brazenly on the top before advancing toward the enemy. His compatriots watched in awe as he strolled toward the Germans. Astonishingly, the Germans carried no visible weapons, and no one shot at their brother-in-arms. More men from both sides made their way toward no-man's land. They greeted each other despite the language barriers. The French side also brought some alcohol and goodies from their stash and shared with the enemy. There was an air of giddiness and frivolity that inversely corresponded to the stress of the warfare and inclement weather.

At some point, one of the Germans produced a football, which they lightheartedly tossed and kicked around. Before the day concluded, at least a couple hundred had taken part in the sporty play. There was no organized game, no chosen sides, probably in taciturn rebellion.

Later that evening, they lit candles and sang *Silent Night,* each in his own language. They had forgotten about the war, at least for a moment.

The following day, orders would come to prevent any such temporary cease-fires from happening again. *Not good for morale.* But to all the soldiers there, the miracle of the Peace of Christ would always be with them.

The notorious *Christmas Truce* came to be regarded as a kind of blip in the customary conduct of wars. Conflicting with the requisite aggressive patriotism, it serves today to exemplify the tremendous contrast between Christianity and war. It highlights High Commands' blood and power lust and its determination to eliminate any temptation to fraternize or empathize with the enemy, in stark contrast to Jesus' call on our lives.

Prayer

Lord, you command us to love our enemies, but how difficult that is! Make our paths clear and show us how to do as you require, please. Give me fortitude to endure the arrows of my enemies and not string my own bow in retaliation. God says that vengeance is His—so help me to believe that, Lord. Amen.

Discussion Questions

1. How did reverence for the true King of kings create a spontaneous cease-fire?

2. How do you think the young soldiers felt the day after Christmas when hostilities started again?

3. What do you think of those who refused to participate in the Christmas "no man's land" celebration, far from home?

Christmas Commissions

1. Enjoy a Christmas Eve dinner with family or friends, or both, and tell each other about the events during the year for which you are grateful to God.
2. Attend a midnight mass or church service.

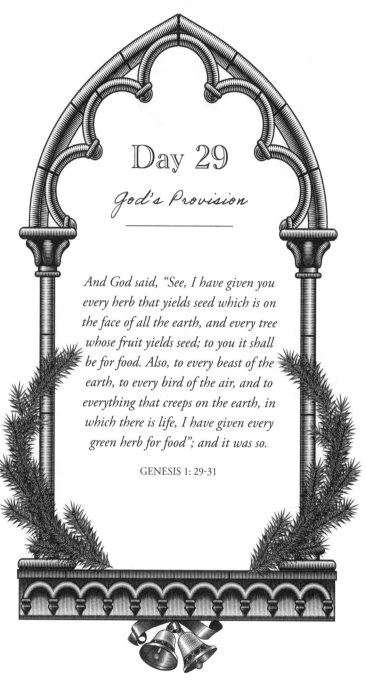

Day 29

God's Provision

And God said, "See, I have given you
every herb that yields seed which is on
the face of all the earth, and every tree
whose fruit yields seed; to you it shall
be for food. Also, to every beast of the
earth, to every bird of the air, and to
everything that creeps on the earth, in
which there is life, I have given every
green herb for food"; and it was so.

GENESIS 1: 29-31

149

The twenty-fifth of December marks the first day of the twelve days of Christmas. At this point in our devotional, now that we have begun the celebration of the holiday itself, we feel called to commemorate more poignantly. Let's delve into the twelve days, first with an examination of the symbols in the song as it relates Christian themes, then with varying hymns themselves, either sung or read aloud as poetry, and then in prayer.

The famous Christmas carol *The Twelve Days of Christmas* goes, "On the first day of Christmas, my true love gave to me a partridge in a pear tree." It's widely held that this singular bird in a tree symbolizes Jesus Christ on the cross. The lyric, in and of itself, makes little sense, as partridges are unlikely to be found in pear trees. They are ground-dwelling and nesting birds, seldom if ever in trees. The idea that Jesus came to dwell on the earth and walk among us also gives credence to the proposed allegory.

Mythology holds that the partridge learned not to fly into trees once the first partridge witnessed Daedalus, in a jealous rage, throwing his apprentice, Talos, off the sacred Athena Hill. From then on, the partridge stayed on the ground.

So, the lyric seems intentionally odd. Some say perhaps "in a pear tree" is a corruption of the French "une perdrix" (pronounced *oohn-pair-dree* and meaning "a partridge"), which would be a repetition of the English word *partridge* but sounds like "in a pear tree."

The partridge is a bird famously known to sacrifice herself for her young. She is, then, an apt representation of Christ, who voluntarily died for the remission of our sins. The pear tree is representative of the cross. While it certainly would be unusual for a partridge to be in a tree, the obvious strangeness of the lyric also points to the unique essence of Christianity. All other religions have a variation of individual performance leading to their version of salvation. Our religion is the only one where salvation is offered freely by another, through His action, not our own. Some people term it like this: other religions are about what you do for God; ours is the reverse. Their religious acolytes say, "This is my body, my choice." Our God says, "This is my body, and it's your choice."

Christ died on a cross made of wood and Christian symbolism often equates the cross to the tree it was crafted from. So that would leave us with the partridge—the motherly bird who sacrifices herself willingly for her offspring, in the pear tree—the cross, which could not hold our savior in death.

Jesus is our provision for the remission of our sins. He generously provides for our needs, just as God provided for Adam and Eve in the Garden of Eden.

God's provision extends to all aspects of our lives, but the most significant is His endowment for our souls. Although He punished the weak and doubting chosen people from the promised land for a full generation, he presented manna from heaven as sustenance for them on their wandering. He always allows a return from our sin. He never fails us.

Jesus said:

> *Look at the birds of the air: they*
> *neither sow nor reap nor gather into*
> *barns, and yet your heavenly Father*
> *feeds them. Are you not of more value*
> *than they?*

(MATTHEW 6:26)

Hymn: *Great Is Thy Faithfulness, O God My Father*
Author: Thomas O. Chisholm (1923)
Tune: *Faithfulness* (Runyan)

1 Great is Thy faithfulness, O God my Father;
   there is no shadow of turning with Thee;
   Thou changest not, Thy compassions, they fail not;
   as Thou hast been, Thou forever wilt be.

   Refrain:
   Great is Thy faithfulness!
   Great is Thy faithfulness!
   Morning by morning new mercies I see;
   all I have needed Thy hand hath provided:
   great is Thy faithfulness, Lord, unto me!

2 Summer and winter, and springtime and harvest;
   sun, moon, and stars in their courses above
   join with all nature in manifold witness
   to Thy great faithfulness, mercy, and love. [*Refrain*]

3 Pardon for sin and a peace that endureth,
   Thine own dear presence to cheer and to guide;

strength for today and bright hope for tomorrow: blessings all mine, with ten thousand beside! [*Refrain*]

Prayer

Lord, please meet me in my feebleness. Your enduring understanding that I know I test with nearly every breath I take, surpasses my weakness and ineptitude. Give me the grace to follow You without exception and take from me the frailty of my heart. Lead me, Lord. Lead me. Amen.

Discussion Questions

1. How does God's provision manifest in our daily lives?

2. What are some ways we can express gratitude for God's deliverance?

3. Can you recall a specific instance where you felt God supernaturally provided for you or someone you know?

Christmas Commission

Call or video call your loved ones who cannot be with you and tell them how much they mean to you.

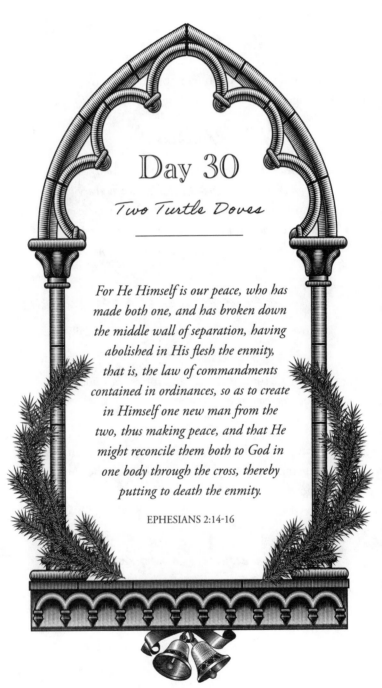

Day 30

Two Turtle Doves

For He Himself is our peace, who has made both one, and has broken down the middle wall of separation, having abolished in His flesh the enmity, that is, the law of commandments contained in ordinances, so as to create in Himself one new man from the two, thus making peace, and that He might reconcile them both to God in one body through the cross, thereby putting to death the enmity.

EPHESIANS 2:14-16

In the tradition of *The Twelve Days of Christmas*, the two turtle doves represent Peace and Unity. Doves are a universal symbol of peace and the pair of them, together, show unity. Ephesians 4:3 reads, "Make every effort to keep the unity of the Spirit through the bond of peace." Active believers should take an emphatic role in preserving unity. Sometimes, during the holiday, it becomes challenging to maintain peace, but this verse reminds us that unity is not passive. It requires intention, effort, and dedication to achieve harmony.

In 1 Corinthians 12:12-14, we find the exhortation to unify in the body of Christ:

> *For as the body is one and has many*
> *members, but all the members of that*
> *one body, being many, are one body,*
> *so also is Christ. For by one Spirit we*
> *were all baptized into one body—*
> *whether Jews or Greeks, whether slaves*
> *or free—and have all been made to*
> *drink into one Spirit. For in fact the*
> *body is not one member but many.*

Christmastime, especially, calls us to come together in purpose—to celebrate the one thing we all have in common, salvation in Jesus Christ. And we recognize that our need for salvation is based entirely on our own sinful nature. So, while I was still a sinner, He died and sacrificed for my sins, and for my brother's. Therefore, let me not cast aspersions on my brother but unite with him in the celebration of our deliverance!

Jesus brings people together, breaking down barriers and creating harmony.

The day after Christmas is commonly known as Boxing Day in the United Kingdom and other British Commonwealth countries. That's decidedly unrelated to anything like the fighting sport or breaking down the gift boxes post-Christmas. In fact, there isn't much to go on for the origins of the phrase, except that it traces back to before 1833, when Charles Dickens used it in *The Pickwick Papers*.

Theories on the origins of the holiday name are connected to charitable efforts. The first idea is that the day after Christmas was reserved to show appreciation to staff who traditionally would have had to work on the Christmas holiday. The day after Christmas, manor lords and aristocrats might "box up" small gifts, money, and Christmas dinner leftovers from the celebration the previous day. These boxes would then be distributed to the staff to enjoy, serving basically as their Christmas bonuses and appreciative acknowledgment of their year-long efforts.

An alternate theory is that churches would have alms boxes in place throughout the season to collect money to help the poor and downtrodden. Once Christmas was over, the contents of the boxes would be distributed by members of the clergy on December 26, which is also known as St. Stephen's Day in honor of the first Christian martyr. He was renowned for his charitable acts.

Consider putting together a box of goodies for a neighbor or a friend in need of some cheer this holiday. It's never too late to show someone some love.

Hymn: *O Come, All Ye Faithful, Joyful and Triumphant*
Author (attributed to): John Francis Wade
Translator: Frederick Oakeley (1841)
Tune: *Adeste Fideles*

1 O come, all ye faithful, joyful and triumphant,
     O come ye, O come ye to Bethlehem!
     Come, and behold Him, born the King of angels!

   Refrain:
     O come, let us adore Him;
     O come, let us adore Him;
     O come, let us adore Him, Christ, the Lord!

2 God of God, Light of Light,
     lo, He abhors not the virgin's womb;
     very God, begotten not created; [*Refrain*]

3 Sing, choirs of angels; sing in exultation;
     sing, all ye citizens of heav'n above!
     Glory to God, all glory in the highest! [*Refrain*]

4 Yea, Lord, we greet Thee, born this happy morning;
     Jesus, to Thee be all glory giv'n!
     Word of the Father, now in flesh appearing! [*Refrain*]

Prayer

Lord, the themes today are unity and peace, but sometimes it's just difficult to overcome my own pettiness and allow others the dignity of their choices. Why do I always feel the need to voice my opinion, even if I know they will disagree? Today, give me the courage and the willfulness to keep quiet, for the sake of peace. Show me how to remain silent without judgment in the face of small disagreements. Guide me away from division and into peace through unity. Amen.

Discussion Questions

1. How does Jesus bring unity among people?

   _____

2. What are some ways we can promote peace in our relationships?

   _____

3. How can we embody peace in our interactions with others?

   _____

Christmas Commission

The Lord's Prayer calls us to forgive others in the same way we seek forgiveness from God. If there is someone in your life who needs your forgiveness and has expressed that to you, offer it. If they are not repentant, offer them forgiveness in your heart and unburden yourself by confessing it to Jesus. If you need to beg someone for their forgiveness, adopt a contrite attitude, and address it with them.

Day 31

Three French Hens

---

*Love suffers long and is kind; love does
not envy; love does not parade itself, is
not puffed up; does not behave rudely,
does not seek its own, is not provoked,
thinks no evil; does not rejoice in
iniquity, but rejoices in the truth;
bears all things, believes all things,
hopes all things, endures all things.
Love never fails.*

1 CORINTHIANS 13:4-8

The three French Hens in *The Twelve Days of Christmas* traditionally represent love, faith, and hope. Each of these is foundational to the Christian walk, like a stool with three legs, sturdy and firm. Reflect on the significance of these qualities in our journey with Christ.

Love is at the seat of our lives. We are relational beings, ill-suited to isolation and needful of companionship. Love is also the reason for Christ. The only aim of His descent from on high to the world below is explained in John 3:16: "For God so loved the world that He gave His only begotten son."

The second pillar is faith. Without faith, there is no religion. A doubter said to a Christian, "If your God is so real, why won't he reveal himself to me? I want to believe, but without actually seeing, how can anyone be expected to just rely on faith?" But we know that if a giant finger were to paint in the sky, "I exist," the doubter would find some other way to explain it, because his default is to not believe in God. Skeptics wish not to know God; therefore, they don't know Him. The famous atheist philosopher Bertrand Russell, upon meeting God and being asked why he could never bring himself to believe in God, despite his intense and forbidding intelligence, would likely answer, "You didn't give me enough proof." But of course, that misses the point, doesn't it? We wouldn't need faith if proof were self-evident like that. It is the mystery of God and the necessity of faith that make our religion real and beautiful. It is the search that makes the treasure worthwhile.

On the flip side, to maintain atheism demands even more faith, arguably, than Christianity. To imagine that nothing came out of nothing to give us everything for no reason and with no scientific explanation is laughable, and yet, that is the atheist's contention.

The third pillar of hope is the source of all happiness. If you were promised a million dollars tomorrow, but also were told you had one week to live, the money wouldn't make you happy. It is only hope that is the seat of our joy. Without hope, in fact, we are as good as lost. They say the main ingredient in happiness is gratitude, but hope is the requisite component. Hope provides the flavoring for the cake, while gratitude is the flour. And hope is the reason He came, because our sin condemns us to misery, but Christ's redemptive act frees us from condemnation and allows us to beg for and receive forgiveness. That's hope.

The French hens are a type of chicken that has blue legs, a white feathered body, and a red comb. Those are the colors of the French flag. They are table birds, prized for their delicate flavor, which is perhaps the reason they are included in a song that is dominated by the breeds of various cooking birds.

The hymn we've chosen to celebrate the second day after Christmas is below. Written by Charles Wesley, who was born on December 18, 1707, in Lincolnshire, England, it is one of over 4,500 hymns penned by the clergyman and poet. In 1726, at the age of 19, he entered Christ Church College, Oxford, and translated Greek and Latin classics into English verse. Two years later, he experienced a spiritual awakening and, together with two other undergraduates, started the Holy Club, in which they shared Holy Communion and pursued serious study of the Bible, as well as visitations to the filthy Oxford prisons. Because of their dogged devotion to scripture and study, they became (derisively) known as "Methodists." His eldest brother, John, joined him in these pursuits, and together they started the Methodist movement in the Church of England. Eventually, Charles left it over differences he had with his brother John. He became a gifted, eloquent preacher, however, and translated the Gospel message into hymns, which became an effective means of evangelism. George Frideric Handel wrote music for many of Wesley's more than 4,500 published hymns. Yes, that's Handel, of *Messiah* (1741) fame.

Hymn: *Hark! The Herald Angels Sing*
Author: Charles Wesley (1739)
Tune: *Mendelssohn* (51171)

1   Hark! the herald angels sing,
     "Glory to the newborn King:
     peace on earth, and mercy mild,
     God and sinners reconciled!"
     Joyful, all ye nations, rise,
     join the triumph of the skies;
     with th'angelic hosts proclaim,
     "Christ is born in Bethlehem!"

Refrain:
Hark! the herald angels sing,
"Glory to the newborn King"

2   Christ, by highest heaven adored,
    Christ, the everlasting Lord,
    late in time behold him come,
    offspring of the Virgin's womb:
    veiled in flesh the Godhead see;
    hail th'incarnate Deity,
    pleased with us in flesh to dwell,
    Jesus, our Immanuel. [*Refrain*]

3   Hail the heaven-born Prince of Peace!
    Hail the Sun of Righteousness!
    Light and life to all he brings,
    risen with healing in his wings.
    Mild he lays his glory by,
    born that we no more may die,
    born to raise us from the earth,
    born to give us second birth. [*Refrain*]

Prayer

Come, Lord Jesus, into my heart. Strengthen my faith and
fill me with hope everlasting. Chase away any doubts I may
have about my future. Lord, You know the past, present, and
future, and You have plans for me from even before I was
born. Let your love shine through me to others and let me be
a beacon of Your mercies, to bring those who don't know You
yet into Your company. Amen.

Discussion Questions

1. How do love, faith, and hope intersect in our lives?

   _____

2. Can you think of examples illustrating each of these qualities?

   _____

3. Why are these qualities essential in our relationship with God and others?

   _____

Christmas Commission

Put on Handel's *Messiah* and sit quietly listening to the entire piece.

Day 32

Four Calling Birds

And He said to them, "Go into
all the world and preach the gospel
to every creature."

MARK 16:15

Originally, in the first known publication of *The Twelve Days of Christmas* in a book called *Mirth Without Mischief*, *Calling* was actually *Colly*. Some folks argue that it makes no sense, while *calling*, in reference to a bird makes perfect sense. It's a songbird, of course, calling to its mate or friends, singing its tune for the world to hear!

But what if that's not the case? Why would the original lyric be written as "Colly"?

This strange word is derivative of *collier*—a coal miner— and *colliery*—a coal mine. Colly referred to anything covered in coal dust, or looking as if it were covered in coal dust. The birds would have been some kind of black bird, though perhaps they might have been the proverbial canaries in the coal mine, who would signify to the miner if the air were too unhealthy for him to continue. Canaries were used to warn of impending danger, like the birds in our song, who are calling out the Gospel. In its own way, the Gospel is a warning to us.

While there are several variations of the song, the lyrical discrepancy has been the source of family debates for over a century. But let's not get caught up in insignificant details, when there are plenty of more important things to discuss. The theme for the day is the proclamation of the Gospel— the Good News. Now, that is something to call out about!

Sharing the Gospel can change lives. To do it well, we need to talk about it honestly and make it understandable for different people. One way to become effective at sharing the Gospel is to learn the various apologetic arguments for it.

C.S. Lewis, an atheist-turned-apologist, offered one of the most effective arguments for the Gospel. He was a tremendously significant and prolific Christian writer, after his conversion to faith. His well-known argument is called the *trilemma,* also known by the phrase, "Liar, Lunatic, or Lord." In his timeless book *Mere Christianity,* he argues,

I am trying here to prevent anyone saying the really foolish thing that people often say about Him: I'm ready to accept Jesus as a great moral teacher, but I don't accept his claim to be God. That is the one thing we must not say. A man who was merely a man and said the sort of things Jesus said would not be a great moral teacher. He would either be a lunatic—on the level with the man who says he is a poached egg—or else he would be the Devil of Hell. You must make your choice. Either this man was, and is, the Son of God, or else a madman or something worse. You can shut him up for a fool, you can spit at him and kill him as a demon or you can fall at his feet and call him Lord and God, but let us not come with any patronizing nonsense about his being a great human teacher. He has not left that open to us. He did not intend to. . . . Now it seems to me obvious that He was neither a lunatic nor a fiend: and consequently, however strange or terrifying or unlikely it may seem, I have to accept the view that He was and is God. *

---

* Lewis, C.S. (1952). *Mere Christianity.* London: Collins. pp. 54–56. In all editions, this is Book II, Chapter 3, "The Shocking Alternative."

There is also the quintilemma, which is easily remembered as an exercise in a Socratic dialog of yes or no questions:

1. Does the New Testament tell the history of Christ?
   a. No—Jesus is a *Legend.*
      i. But the Bible is unrefuted throughout time and is corroborated by disinterested historians of the day.
   b. Yes—go to #2
2. Did Jesus say He was God?
   a. No—Jesus was just a *Lama.*
      i. But, in the uncontested Bible, Jesus makes many claims, including that He is the Son of God who sits at the right hand of the Father.
   b. Yes—go to #3
3. Did Jesus mean for us to believe He was God?
   a. No—Jesus was a *Lunatic.*
      i. Jesus made it very clear that He intended for us to believe He was "The way, the truth, and the life."
   b. Yes—go to #4
4. Then, Jesus is God?
   a. No—Jesus was a *Liar.*
      i. A liar, personally known and believed by many who, persecuted for it, never wavered in their faith—unto death.
   b. Yes—Jesus is *Lord!*

Once you have these four questions down—really you only need to memorize the five L word choices to discuss with someone—you can start sharing the Good News right away! Sharing the Gospel helps us connect with others and bring faith and community together. So, perhaps don't be a colly bird, but be a calling bird, instead.

Hymn: *The First Noel, The Angel Did Say*
Author: Anonymous (1833)
Tune: *The First Nowell*

1 The first Noel the angel did say
   was to certain poor shepherds in fields as they lay,
   in fields where they lay keeping their sheep,
   on a cold winter's night that was so deep.

   Refrain:
   Noel, Noel, Noel, Noel,
   born is the King of Israel.

2 They looked up and saw a star
   shining in the east beyond them far;
   and to the earth it gave great light,
   and so it continued both day and night. [*Refrain*]

3 And by the light of that same star
   three wise men came from country far;
   to seek for a king was their intent,
   and to follow the star wherever it went. [*Refrain*]

4 This star drew nigh to the northwest;
   o'er Bethlehem it took its rest,
   and there it did both stop and stay,
   right over the place where Jesus lay. [*Refrain*]

5 Then entered in those wise men three,
   full reverently upon their knee,

and offered there in his presence
their gold, and myrrh, and frankincense. [*Refrain*]

6 Then let us all with one accord
sing praises to our heavenly Lord,
that hath made heaven and earth of nought,
and with his blood our life hath bought. [*Refrain*]

Prayer

Father Abba, help erase my timidity, and give me boldness to proclaim Your lordship over my life. Your Son said those who are ashamed of him, he would deny before You, so let me not be one of those, but let me be strong in my faith and my testimony. Please show me how to share, create opportunities for me to bear witness, and thank you for Your Son. Amen.

Discussion Questions

1. Why is it important to share the Gospel?

   _____

2. What challenges might we face when proclaiming the Gospel?

   _____

3. What is one way you can share your faith with an unbeliever today? Remember, small things can impact in a big way.

   _____

Christmas Commissions

1. Buy someone in line behind you their drink or a treat at the coffee shop.
2. Leave some quarters in vending machine change returns for others to find!

Day 33

Five Golden Rings

---

*Every good gift and every perfect gift is
from above, and comes down from the
Father of lights, with whom there is no
variation or shadow of turning.*

JAMES 1:17

The five golden rings likely don't indicate any kind of jewelry; rather they denote either the yellowish rings on the neck of a pheasant, or they might refer to the *goldspinks,* the old name for the bright little birds we call *goldfinches* today. That would make better sense than jewelry, as all the other initial seven gifts are types of birds in the song. Ultimately, many like to tie the number five to the Pentateuch, the first five books of the Old Testament.

A December 20, 2022 article in the *New York Post* recounts the Canadian astrophysicist Dr. Anna Hughes tweeting her discovery of the possible genesis of the rings to be those on a pheasant's neck. According to one reader, upon sharing the article out loud, her partner shouted, "No!" as if her words had just cancelled Christmas, forever. Another reader quipped, "I'm starting to think this 'True Love' is just a cat bringing their kills back to their owner's porch."

All joking aside, however, consider why some might be so beholden to their traditional understanding of the song. Once we learn something as children, it is difficult to unseat, because if a deeply held belief is called into question, well, it calls all our other long-standing notions into question, which is unsettling and makes us vulnerable. But, in Christ, we are conquerors.

Catarina grew up in a two-parent home and graduated high school near the top of her class. Her older parents had waited a long time to have a child and they devoted a lot of their time to helping her excel. She loved them for it. She was an over-achiever, graduating *suma cum laude* from Princeton University and continuing in the PhD program in non-linear mathematics.

For Christmas, she decided to try one of those ancestry tests that tell you about your bloodline. The results arrived by mail on the Thursday before Christmas and she was excited to share them with her folks. She put them on top of her suitcase and drove the five-plus hours back home, happy to have something fun to show her folks when she got there.

The drive was perilous and took much longer than anticipated, with a light snow dusting the icy roads, and she was exhausted when she finally came through the door. Mom and Dad had waited up to see her and it was a sweet, though tired, reunion. She went to bed and didn't think of the envelope until she pulled it out of the pocket of her luggage the next morning.

When she came down for breakfast, still holding the envelope, the smell of coffee leapt into her nostrils, and the sizzling bacon had her taste buds firing. "Good morning! I have a surprise for you guys," Catarina sang, producing the envelope with a flourish. "Merry Christmas! I decided to run my blood for an ancestry panel!"

"What?" Mom turned quickly from the stove, holding a plate. She looked at Dad as Catarina continued.

"It's one of those ancestry things that tells you who your forefathers are. I know we have our family tree, mainly, but I thought this could help fill in some blanks," she said, tearing the envelope open.

She read the results silently, as Mom and Dad just looked at her, their horror and shame burning quietly from their chests up to their throats. They were pinned down by a secret they had never had the courage the share, and now they were about to be undone by a single sheet of paper in their daughter's hand.

Catarina's results showed her to be fully Scandinavian, but she knew both her parents traced their genealogy back several generations in only the Slovakian countries. "It says I'm one hundred percent Swedish. But you both have never said anything about Swedish ancestry. This makes no sense, right?" she said. She looked up at them both.

Mom and Dad were looking at each other. With a nod they said, in unison, "You're adopted."

Catarina's whole world shifted. She stood up. "What?" Then she sat back down again, confounded. "But. . . . "

Dad interrupted her. "Sweetheart, it was never the right time to tell you. And your birth parents passed away. Your mother died in childbirth, sadly, and we got notice of your father passing away when you were still very young."

Catarina's mother quickly interjected, "We were so lucky to get you!"

Catarina looked from Dad to Mom and back again. "You know what this means?"

Her parents stared blankly at her, expecting their world to crumble like meringue in a hurricane. Dad said, "We love you very much. You know that, right?"

Catarina smiled with tears in her eyes. "Wow! This is incredible and humbling news! Wow! You guys think I'm mad? Upset? No! No, I'm not."

Her parents looked at each other for a moment. Mom started to cry.

"Wait . . ." she said, more to herself, subconsciously trying to hit pause on her mother's emotions. "I'm trying to digest this . . . but really, does it make a difference? I suppose, for medical reasons, maybe a tiny bit. But honestly, I'm the luckiest girl in the world. I mean, you guys, Mom, Dad, I love you both so much."

Mom, tears streaming, gushed, "I'm so sorry this happened this way. We never wanted to hurt you. . . . "

Catarina's father jumped in with, "We never knew how to tell you. . . . "

"Right! And now, you don't have to! It's amazing."

Dad said, "I guess it is. If there's anything else you want to know, we will fill in any blanks that we can."

"Yes. Okay. No. I'm so blessed, and this answers a few things for me, anyway. But one thing is for sure—I'm so blessed to have you guys for parents! Praise God and Merry Christmas, Mom and Dad!"

Hymn: *Angels We Have Heard on High*
Tune: *Gloria* (French)

1 Angels we have heard on high,
   sweetly singing o'er the plains,
   and the mountains in reply
   echoing their joyous strains:

   Refrain:
   Gloria, in excelsis Deo!
   Gloria, in excelsis Deo!

2 Shepherds, why this jubilee?
  Why your joyous strains prolong?
  What the gladsome tidings be
  which inspire your heav'nly song? [*Refrain*]

3 Come to Bethlehem and see
  Him whose birth the angels sing;
  come, adore on bended knee
  Christ the Lord, the new-born King. [*Refrain*]

4 See Him in a manger laid,
  Jesus, Lord of heav'n and earth!
  Mary, Joseph, lend your aid,
  sing with us our Savior's birth. [*Refrain*]

Prayer

My Pappa in Heaven, help me to reflect on the various blessings You've bestowed on me, considering my failures and lack of deservedness. Humble me to count them as only testimony to Your greatness and not of my own doing. I pray for blessings to be showered down upon those around me and for humility to overtake my ego. Amen.

Discussion Questions:

1. What blessings have you received from God?

   _____

2. How does acknowledging God's blessings impact our perspective?

   _____

3. How can we share our blessings with others?

   _____

Christmas Commission

Offer to serve at your church to give those who worked over the holiday a break.

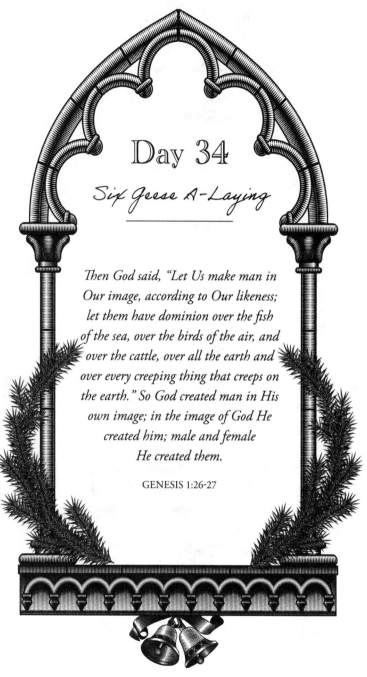

Day 34

Six Geese A-Laying

Then God said, "Let Us make man in
Our image, according to Our likeness;
let them have dominion over the fish
of the sea, over the birds of the air, and
over the cattle, over all the earth and
over every creeping thing that creeps on
the earth." So God created man in His
own image; in the image of God He
created him; male and female
He created them.

GENESIS 1:26-27

179

The lyric of the song being six geese laying eggs is reference to the days of Creation, when God "hatched" or formed the universe, the world, and all things in it.

Day one: God created the heavens and the earth.
Day two: God created the sky and the seas.
Day three: God created the land and plants.
Day four: God created the sun, moon, and stars,
Day five: God created the fish and birds.
Day six: God created land animals and man.
Day seven: God rested!

What came first, the goose or the egg? God came first—and that resolves that dilemma for all time, because God creates whatever He desires, and it doesn't matter in what stage it appears to Him, as He is outside of time itself. In fact, the phrase in the Genesis in which God speaks light into being, *yehi 'ohr*, indicates desire. But the Hebrew word for light, *ohr*, also translates in a sense to time itself. Perhaps a more appropriate translation of the phrase "Let there be light" in the Bible is "Begin!" and that's how God set the wheels of time, space, and light in motion.

In our movie, *Let There Be Light,* Sol Harkins has a near-death experience and gets a message from his deceased son, comprising those four words. Kevin's film character goes on a journey of discovery of what those words might mean. At first, he is simply confounded. As an avowed atheist, Sol cannot comprehend why he would have seen *anything* when he flirted with death. The hospital pronounced him dead for four minutes and for Sol, as he expresses in the initial debate that opens the film, death is the end and then there is nothing.

So, why would he see *something*?

Sol's entire worldview was being shattered and all his firm-set beliefs were crumbling. Lucky for him, he had somewhere to turn. His ex-wife, Katy, a believer, had long since given up trying to convince Sol that life was worth living because God ruled the world. The loss of their little boy had proved just too much for a man without faith. The grief that couldn't be resolved had eaten him up from the inside and produced in Sol a self-destructive streak that was slowly taking over his entire life. From the drinking to the pill-popping to the dangerous social behavior, Sol's life was careening out of control, to the point that his car accident was ultimately no accident, but simply a natural consequence of all that preceded it.

Waking up in the hospital with barely a mark on him, Sol has an epiphany from his new revelation. If his dead son can talk to him from beyond the grave, there must *be* a beyond, and that changes everything.

After that, Sol explores many different explanations for why he glimpsed the little boy whose death eventually precipitated Sol's life-crisis. As a last resort, Sol finally meets with Katy's pastor, a mafia boss who turned state's witness, served time, and found Christ inside his jail cell. His character's story in the movie is the true story of Michael Franzese, who played Pastor Vinnie in real life. In fact, the prisoner number that Vinnie gives in the movie, to prove to Sol he's the real deal, was Michael's number in Lompoc prison.

Pastor Vinnie shares with Sol that God is patient and requires nothing more than that you open the door to Him. Just let Him in, and He will do the rest. Pursue Him, and He will pursue you back. "Let there be light" is an imperative to let the light and love of Christ shine into you and then through you to the world. Can you do that?

We often run from the truth, like Sol. We construct a world around us that we think satisfies our needs, only to discover, sometimes too late, that our efforts cannot possibly match those of the God of the universe. Sol had crafted a world in which he was the center. He did what he wanted, when he wanted it. He was angry at the loss of his son, nihilistic in his approach to living, undisciplined and debauched. Was it fun? In the moment, perhaps, but at the end of the day his life was without hope—the essential ingredient for happiness. Fun without happiness is like a smile that doesn't rise to the eyes, insincere and eerie.

Sol had become a shell of a man, mirthless and cynical, and it took the love of Christ to set him back on his path. The movie ends at Christmas, with lights shining up to the heavens from all over the world, and Sol, having come a full one-eighty, loving God for making life so indescribably beautiful, and for His promise that the end is just the beginning.

Hymn: *All Creatures of Our God and King*
Paraphraser: William H. Draper; Author: St. Francis of
Assisi (1225)
Tune: *Lasst Uns Erfreuen*

1 All creatures of our God and King,
   lift up your voice and with us sing,
   "Alleluia! Alleluia!"
   Thou burning sun with golden beam,
   thou silver moon with softer gleam,
   O praise Him, O praise Him!
   alleluia, alleluia, alleluia!

2 Thou rushing wind that art so strong,
   ye clouds that sail in heav'n along,
   O praise Him! Alleluia!
   Thou rising morn, in praise rejoice,
   ye lights of ev'ning, find a voice,
   O praise Him, O praise Him!
   alleluia, alleluia, alleluia!

3 And all ye men of tender heart,
   forgiving others, take your part,
   O sing ye! Alleluia!
   Ye who long pain and sorrow bear,
   praise God and on Him cast your care;
   O praise Him, O praise Him!
   alleluia, alleluia, alleluia!

4 Let all things their Creator bless,
   and worship Him in humbleness;
   O praise Him! Alleluia!

Praise, praise the Father, praise the Son,
and praise the Spirit, Three in One;
O praise Him, O praise Him!
alleluia, alleluia, alleluia!
alleluia, alleluia, alleluia!

Prayer

May I be a vessel for the love of Christ to shine through to the world around me. May I carry the message of the love of God for His creation. May I die to my own ego but live in Christ Jesus this holiday. Thank you, God, for hearing my prayers. Amen.

Discussion Questions

1. What does it mean to be a steward of God's creation?

   _____

2. How does being a steward project God's light on others around us?

   _____

3. When did you first sense the freedom from knowing God was in control?

   _____

Christmas Commission

Write thank-you notes for your gifts and include some description of how important the gift-giver is to you.

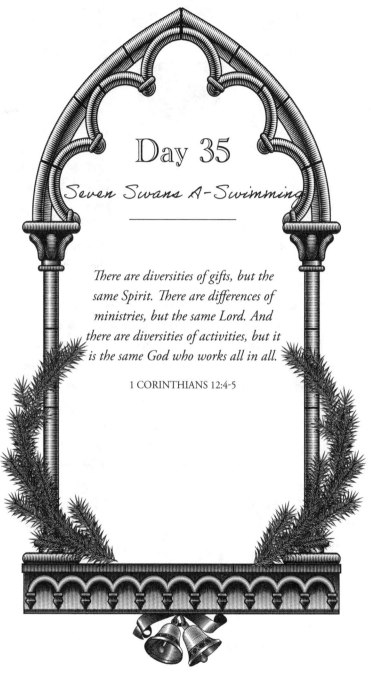

Day 35

Seven Swans A-Swimming

There are diversities of gifts, but the
same Spirit. There are differences of
ministries, but the same Lord. And
there are diversities of activities, but it
is the same God who works all in all.

1 CORINTHIANS 12:4-5

In our famous song *The Twelve Days of Christmas*, "seven swans a-swimming" refers distinctly to the seven gifts of the Holy Spirit, as delineated by Paul in both Romans and 1st Corinthians: wisdom, understanding, counsel, fortitude, knowledge, piety, and fear of the Lord.

Constance was a quiet, shy young girl who loved to draw. Her mother bought her a paint set when she realized her daughter's predilection, a great big colorful set that came in a large cardboard box, and inside were its own wooden box, a palette, and several different types of brushes. They went to the local art store to pick out some canvases. Constance was too embarrassed to tell her mother that she worried that the paints were not very high-quality. She always endeavored to smooth rather than ruffle feathers.

In the store, they ran into Kree and her mother.

The girls jumped together, excited to happen upon each other there. Constance took Kree's hand and led her to the paint's aisle. "Kree, I wanted to show you! Look what my mother bought me as an early Christmas gift—it's at home, but they still have them over here." She pointed to the brightly colored box that sat on the lowest shelf in front of them.

Kree bent down and tried lifting the box. "This one?" she asked, grunting from the weight.

"I know. Isn't it great? We just came in to pick up a canvas or two."

"You're so lucky, Con! I wish I had half your talent."

"You want to come over and we can paint together?"

"I would, but mine won't be half as pretty as yours. . . ."

"It's not a contest!"

They decided to get together that weekend at Constance's house, so Constance's mother bought a few extra canvases. On the way home, she asked Constance, "Did you want to maybe invite Tessa and Michelle, too? I'm sure they'd love to paint, too."

Although Constance had known Tessa and Michelle since first grade, high school had shifted personalities. While, as young girls, they had done playdates, American Heritage Girls, and field trips together, in junior high and high school an arrogance seemed to overtake the pair, at least to Constance. They ran hot and cold and she never knew where she stood with them.

Her mother said that young women were often catty and fickle, but their behavior seemed to go beyond that description. At one moment, they might hug Constance, but at another, randomly, they snubbed her. One day they all met up for lunch and shared their lunches with each other. Another day, Constance sat down with them, only to have them both stand up and announce they were going to take a walk together, leaving Constance sitting alone. She never knew how to behave around them because she could never quite anticipate their attitudes or actions.

"Mm. I think it'll be just fine for just me and Kree, Mom. I don't need the extra distraction. We really want to paint, so. . . . " She let her voice trail off, hoping that might be the end of the discussion.

"Well, I just thought. . . . "

Constance interrupted her. "I've figured out, Mom, that I'm an introvert."

"No, you're not! Don't be ridiculous!"

"You're not thinking of it the right way, Mom. An introvert is someone who gets drained being around other people. I just don't care enough to spend time with most people. They wear me out."

"But you go to school every day!"

"Yeah. And it's exhausting! Listen, they are nice enough, but they just aren't my cup of tea. You love to be around people—I don't. It's that simple."

"Okay." Mom was upset but didn't know how to argue with Constance's logic. If Constance was convinced, who was she to protest—and what good would it do, anyway?

A few days later, Constance had set up the paints on the screened-in porch. The weather was warm, even for Florida in December, and a soft breeze was blowing, but the two girls were well-shaded by the tall hedges on one side.

They concentrated hard on their canvases for two hours. Kree finally finished an unskilled picture of flowers in a sunset. The colors were soothing and attractive, even if her artistic talents weren't quite developed.

Mom emerged with hot chocolate just as Kree walked over to Constance.

Constance's canvas was a study in opposites: a realistically depicted young girl's face breaking apart into puzzle pieces that floated off into a cloudy sky. It was mesmerizing and intriguing. Kree walked over as Constance stepped back to study the work she had begun two days before, unconvinced that she had finished.

"Wow! That's amazing. You're so talented, Con. It's captivating. I can't look away."

"Yes," said her mother softly.

"Mm. I'm not sure it's done. I like it, but I don't know, yet, either."

"You're such a perfectionist. You need to relax a bit. I'm giving mine to my mother for Christmas."

"That's a beautiful gift, Kree," Mom said.

"Only if you don't show her yours!" Kree said to Constance, nudging her in the ribs.

"Don't say that. We all have different giftings."

"Yeah. That's true," Kree said.

Constance's mother thought of God's blessings and how they shower everyone so differently.

Hymn: *A Mighty Fortress Is Our God*
Author: Martin Luther (1529)
Tune: *Ein Feste Burg*

1 A mighty fortress is our God,
   a trusty shield and weapon;
   he helps us free from ev'ry need
   that has us now o'ertaken.
   The old evil foe
   now means deadly woe;
   deep guile and great might
   are his dread arms in fight;
   on earth is not his equal.

2 With might of ours can naught be done,
   soon were our loss effected;

but for us fights the valiant one
whom God himself elected.
You ask, "Who is this?"
Jesus Christ it is,
the almighty Lord,
and there's no other God;
he holds the field forever.

3 Though devils all the world should fill,
all eager to devour us,
we tremble not, we fear no ill:
they shall not overpow'r us.
This world's prince may still
scowl fierce as he will,
he can harm us none.
He's judged; the deed is done;
one little word can fell him.

4 The Word they still shall let remain
nor any thanks have for it;
he's by our side upon the plain
with his good gifts and Spirit.
And take they our life,
goods, fame, child, and wife,
though all may be gone,
our victory is won;
the kingdom's ours forever!

Prayer

Lord, give me patience to understand other people's points of view and experiences. Give me tools to come alongside those for whom I might be useful. Let me bless others and fully appreciate the blessing you've bestowed on me. Amen.

Discussion Questions

1. What are the gifts of the Holy Spirit mentioned in this passage?

   _____

2. How can we use our spiritual gifts to benefit others?

   _____

3. Why is it important for the church to operate using these diverse gifts?

   _____

Christmas Commissions

1. Decide to read through the entire Bible in a year. There are plenty of study guides for this. Reserve time each morning or night and start a new habit!
2. Invite some friends over to do a short Bible study. Use the verse above to spur a conversation about various gifts and what they mean or can be used for.

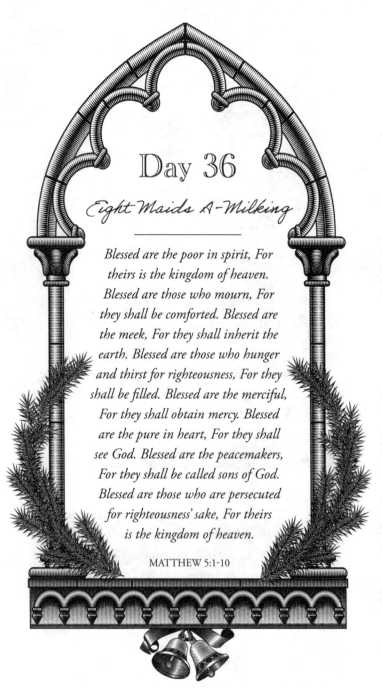

Day 36

Eight Maids A-Milking

Blessed are the poor in spirit, For theirs is the kingdom of heaven. Blessed are those who mourn, For they shall be comforted. Blessed are the meek, For they shall inherit the earth. Blessed are those who hunger and thirst for righteousness, For they shall be filled. Blessed are the merciful, For they shall obtain mercy. Blessed are the pure in heart, For they shall see God. Blessed are the peacemakers, For they shall be called sons of God. Blessed are those who are persecuted for righteousness' sake, For theirs is the kingdom of heaven.

MATTHEW 5:1-10

The eight maids in the song would have been meaningful, as milk was an important ingredient in any Christmas feast. From the Christian perspective, they indicate the eight beatitudes Jesus spoke in His Sermon on the Mount, which are listed above.

Treat walked into The Roundup ready to dance. Tuesday was his one night off, and with the holiday coming, he'd been picking up extra hours at the club where he was a bouncer. He ordered a water at the bar and turned to watch the floor. It was packed with country dancers having fun. Brooks and Dunn's *Boot Scootin' Boogie* was blasting. Treat tapped his toe and looked around for a prospective dance partner. The girls were dressed to impress in cut-offs and tank tops, hats and kerchiefs, and of course, cowboy boots. He watched the more serious ones for someone with experience, because he knew the only way he'd improve was to dance with girls better than he, and those gals were becoming increasingly difficult to find.

Tricia, five-foot six, muscular, with a wide, bright smile, seemed to fit the bill. She was line dancing with a few others, but her moves were smooth, graceful, and polished.

The song ended and she walked over to the bar with her posse, laughing.

They were going to sit this song out, so Treat decided to take a turn line dancing for the next song. As he danced, he called out a few of the simpler directions for the novices dancing next to him, who appreciated it as they stepped on each other's toes. "Now to the right," he said, "Forward three and back again."

The song ended and he caught Tricia's eye and smiled. He made his way over to her. "You look like someone who two-steps. Would you like to dance?"

She giggled and looked at her girlfriends, like there were some inside joke. "Ah . . . sure. This your first time at Roundup?"

"As a matter of fact, it's been a while since I've been up this way. I usually dance at a bar further south, but I had to come up this way, so I thought I'd try it out."

"Uh huh," she answered as they began to dance. Treat was a solid dancer, fluid, with strength, and as he led her on the dance floor, she was clearly pleased, enjoying herself. He dipped her at the finale for the song, then lifted her effortlessly back up.

"Thank you, Ma'am."

"Ma'am? Who are you, my lawyer?" she giggled. "Doesn't matter," she added before he could answer, "You're pretty good!"

"Thanks. Wanna try another song?"

"No, she sure doesn't," said a guy taking Tricia's arm and pulling her back to stand between her and Treat. He was about an inch taller than treat and obviously a bodybuilder. He seemed to be looking for a fight, jutting his chin out, with a challenge in his glare.

"Whoa, Dude, it was just a dance. No harm done." Treat held his hands up as if surrendering, but the guy wasn't buying it.

"Jake, it was just a dance. You weren't even here. Just one dance!" Tricia implored.

Jake turned to her and said, "I'll thank you to shut your pretty little mouth." He turned back to Treat and said, "You wanna take this outside?"

Treat started laughing. He could take this guy to the cleaners, with all his training in both martial arts and just in handling bullies through his job. He could teach this guy a lesson he'd never forget, and the guy certainly was deserving. Then again, he thought, *Discretion is the better part of valor.* Ruining both their nights and leaving the guy without any dignity because he didn't know better than to pick a fight with Treat wasn't the way to play this. Treat's pastor defined meekness, a quality that Jesus obviously prized, as power under control. The superior plan would be to diffuse the situation.

"Look, man, this is between you and your girl. We don't need to fight about it. All I did was ask her to dance because she seemed unattached. We had a dance, and now we're done. Ask her friends, there. Your honor is still intact, and so is hers, and I'll just walk away, if it's all right with you."

Jake continued the stand-off, trying to calculate—based on Treat's self-assuredness—the best course.

Treat figured it couldn't hurt to hurry him along. "You good?" Power under control. Treat put his hand out and Jake couldn't help but shake it and smile.

"Sure, bro. We're good. We're cool."

Hymn: *Holy, Holy, Holy*
Author: Reginald Heber (1826)
Tune: *Nicaea*

1 Holy, holy, holy! Lord God Almighty!
   Early in the morning our song shall rise to Thee;
   Holy, holy, holy! merciful and mighty!
   God in three Persons, blessed Trinity!

2 Holy, holy, holy! All the saints adore Thee,
   casting down their golden crowns around the glassy sea;
   cherubim and seraphim, falling down before Thee,
   which wert and art and evermore shalt be.

3 Holy, holy, holy! Though the darkness hide Thee,
   though the eye of sinful man Thy glory may not see;
   only Thou art holy, there is none beside Thee,
   perfect in pow'r, in love, and purity.

4 Holy, holy, holy! Lord God Almighty!
   All Thy works shall praise Thy name, in earth and sky
      and sea;
   Holy, holy, holy! merciful and mighty!
   God in three Persons, blessed Trinity!

Prayer

God, sometimes I'm just a hothead. I react too quickly, too rashly. Lord, help me to learn patience. Help me to be more like You, meek, understanding the power you have but reluctant to utilize it. Force seldom solves problems as well as charm, so dwell inside me and train me in Your ways, instead of my own. Amen.

Discussion Questions

1. Why would both Moses and Jesus claim they were meek men?

   _____

2. How does being meek differ from being weak?

   _____

3. Read the Beatitudes and discuss how they turned the world's expectations on its head.

   _____

Christmas Commission

Find a good commentary on the Beatitudes and discover the less-obvious meanings behind each of them. Try putting this new knowledge to good use in your daily life.

Day 37

Nine Ladies Dancing

Shout joyfully to the Lord,
all the earth;

Break forth in song, rejoice,
and sing praises.

Sing to the Lord with the harp,

With the harp and the sound
of a psalm,

With trumpets and the sound
of a horn;

Shout joyfully before the Lord,
the King.

PSALM 98:4-6

198

The nine ladies dancing are meant to represent the fruit of the spirit.

> *But the fruit of the Spirit is love,*
> *joy, peace, longsuffering, kindness,*
> *goodness, faithfulness, gentleness, self-*
> *control. Against such there is no law.*

GALATIANS 5:22-23

Cody was annoyed at his little sister.

He had promised to drive her to her book club, and she had assured him he didn't need to worry about when to pick her up because she had a ride to tennis practice, but then it turned out that she needed a ride home from tennis! What could she possibly have meant that he needn't consider picking her back up, except that she had a ride back home *after* tennis. Now, he had to drive out in the rain to go get her, because tennis was rained out and she was stuck.

That wasn't such a big deal, except for not being able to rely on his sister to effectively communicate, but he had invited Brian over to play Pokémon GO and now this changed their plans. He hated that someone else could dictate his schedule. That really bugged him. Brian was due any minute. In fact, there was his white Ford truck pulling in the driveway.

Cody met Brian at the door. "Hey. Listen, uhm, my baby sister needs a ride, so I have to go get her. I'm really sorry to bail like this, but she just called and never told me about needing a ride home. I feel bad about the Pokémon."

Brian looked around, measuring his response. His laid-back demeanor and the casual flop of bangs hiding his left eye belied his serious nature. "Dang. Well. . . . How about I ride with you, since I'm already here?"

"Nah . . . it'd be an imposition. You could go play, anyway, and I'll meet up with you later. I mean, it's twenty-five minutes there and then another back again."

"So? It's no big thing. I'll ride along and keep you company."

Cody reached inside for his wallet and keys, saying, "It's your funeral."

As they drove, the skies cleared.

"Look. It's clearing up!"

"Toldja you should've just gone to the park on your own."

"Dude, I just thought riding together would be more fun for both of us. Is that your sister there?" he continued, pointing out a tall, gangly fourteen-year-old in shorts and a T-shirt.

Cody pulled over.

"Thanks, Cody! I figured the least I could do was wait outside, now that the rain has stopped," said Lara as she got in the car.

Cody, still in a bad mood, answered, "Yes. The very least."

Brian said, "Nice to see you, Lara. I came along for the ride."

Lara said, "I saw that. Super cool, thanks. Hey, isn't there a really good Pokémon GO park near here? I don't mind if you guys want to walk it for a while. I'll just read or whatever while you play. I'm dressed warmly enough."

Brian looked at Cody. "She's right. Granger Park is just down the street that way and it's a good one for the game. I say we go there for an hour."

Cody smiled. "If it's not too cold for Lara, then I'm in!" he said gleefully, taking the next right turn and heading straight for the park.

After about an hour and a half, the young men picked up Lara, who was seated on a park bench near the car, and they started back home, chatting about the various Pokémon they had succeeded in finding. Five minutes into their drive, Brian said, "Who wants shaved ice? I'm buying. Merry Christmas!"

"Seriously?!" asked Lara. "I'm in!"

Cody said, "It's cold out, but you're gonna eat shaved ice?"

Lara answered, cutting Cody off, "Don't be such a negative Nellie, Codes. I'll do a shaved with vanilla ice cream inside!"

Brian said, "C'mon, *Codes,* the place is right up there on the left. I'll get you any flavor you want. Plus, the car is heated."

Cody thought about it for a few seconds. "Brian," he asked, "How do you always manage to have a good time, despite the circumstances? I never see you upset. . . ."

"Oh, I get upset. I just choose my battles carefully," answered Brian, looking back toward Lara in the back seat and smiling. "Happiness is a choice, so I choose it. Why grumble about things I can't change?"

Cody chewed on that until they found a parking space, far from the entrance to the Rosy's Icies. "This place is packed with Christmas shoppers!"

"Isn't it great?" exclaimed Brian, gleefully.

Cody looked at him and checked himself. He wasn't sure why his attitude always veered contrary, but he vowed right then and there that the better way forward was to try a more positive attitude. He got out of the car and said, "Race you inside!"

Lara let out a surprised yelp and started running after him, with Brian gaining from behind.

Hymn: *Joy to the World*
Author: Isaac Watts (1719)
Tune: *Antioch* (Handel)

1 Joy to the world, the Lord is come!
   Let earth receive her King!
   Let every heart prepare Him room,
   and heav'n and nature sing,
   and heav'n and nature sing,
   and heav'n, and heav'n and nature sing.

2 Joy to the earth, the Savior reigns!
   Let men their songs employ,
   while fields and floods, rocks, hills, and plains
   repeat the sounding joy,
   repeat the sounding joy,
   repeat, repeat the sounding joy.

3 No more let sins and sorrows grow,
   nor thorns infest the ground;
   He comes to make His blessings flow
   far as the curse is found,

far as the curse is found,
far as, far as the curse is found.

4 He rules the world with truth and grace,
and makes the nations prove
the glories of His righteousness
and wonders of His love,
and wonders of His love,
and wonders, wonders of His love.

Prayer

Lord, lead me into gratitude for each and every day, for every blessing and every trial, for every up and every down. Lord, help me appreciate that without the lows there could be no highs, and without sadness, happiness would lose its luster. So, I thank You for all of it, and not just some of it. Amen.

Discussion Questions

1. What brings joy to your life?

_____

2. How can celebrations express our gratitude to God?

_____

3. How does joy in the Lord differ from happiness?

_____

Christmas Commission

Find someone in your neighborhood to bless, unexpectedly, whether it's bringing them a cup of coffee or a bouquet of flowers or offering to drive them somewhere. Find a need and serve another.

Day 38

Ten Lords A-Leeping

Stand fast therefore in the liberty
by which Christ has made us free,
and do not be entangled again
with a yoke of bondage.

GALATIONS 5:1

Lords were also considered judges and therefore in charge of the law. Ten lords in action, as the song lyric in *The Twelve Days of Christmas* references, represent the ten commandments:

1. Thou shall have no other gods before me.
2. Thou shalt not make unto thee any graven image.
3. Thou shalt not take the name of the Lord thy God in vain.
4. Remember the Sabbath Day to keep it holy.
5. Honor they father and mother.
6. Thou shalt not kill.
7. Thou shalt not commit adultery.
8. Thou shalt not steal.
9. Thou shalt not bear false witness.
10. Thou shalt not covet.

Jed's group of guys all planned to go to a friend's cabin up at the lake for a fun overnight, and he was the designated driver. Jed had always been a responsible kid. He worked a ton of odd jobs from an early age and had saved nearly every penny. When he turned sixteen, on his birthday, he got his license and then immediately went to buy himself a used car with his savings. He was just itching for his independence.

The morning he was supposed to go pick up his buddies, his dad called him into the kitchen before he headed out. "They're saying there's a big storm heading our way tonight."

"I'm not worried. Dad, they're just fearmongering. It'll probably blow right through and barely leave a dusting." Jed shook his head and shrugged, making light of the cold weather prediction.

"Well, let's hope so, but just in case, you better not head up to the lake. You never know what the roads'll be like up there, especially with fresh snow."

The lake was more of a summer place, but there was a magical quiet to the area in winter, and this trip boasted an added incentive of spending time away from home with his buddies—being independent for a night.

It struck Jed that his father could easily just shut the whole thing down, and that was the last thing Jed wanted.

"Don't worry, Dad. We'll be super careful, and my car has winter tires on, so it'll be safe."

"I don't like the forecast, though. I really think you should just postpone for a day or two."

"Dad, Chris is leaving town the day after tomorrow, so it won't be the same thing. I'm gonna be late. . . ."

"Jed, I do not want you to make this drive! You're a new driver and it's too dangerous!" His father was serious.

"Okay, Dad! Jeese! I'm gonna be late! Don't wait up!" Jed slammed out of the house, angry. Jed hated all the rules his parents had for him. He loved his parents, but they sure could get on his last nerve.

He met up with his friends at Chris's house. Chris had been Jed's friend since kindergarten, and they were very close. Chris picked up his duffel to load it into the car.

"My dad told me he didn't want me driving up to the lake tonight, because of the potential for a storm. Can you believe that?"

"I didn't see any storm predictions," replied Chris. "Look at the sky. It's clear. If we hurry, we'll get there before any weather moves in, anyway, right?"

Jed didn't disobey his parents easily, but in this case, he just knew his dad was wrong. He was nearly a grown man, now, with a driver's license and his own car. Why shouldn't he be able to decide what was best for himself?

Jed and Chris picked up their two other friends on the way and soon they were driving out to the lake house. The almost two-hour drive was longer because halfway there, a nasty storm moved in from out of nowhere and enveloped the car in a white-out. To make matters worse, they missed the country road turn-off the first time by, and then passed it again on the way back. By the time they realized their mistake and turned around again, the storm had grown fierce, but they were determined to get where they intended.

After taking the turn-off for the two-lane lake road, Jed soon realized the flurries swirling in the frigid wind created such reflections that seeing more than ten feet in front of the windshield became nearly impossible. Pretty soon, he was driving five miles per hour and scared he might accidentally run off the road.

Erik spoke up from the back seat, "You drive like an old lady!"

Paul snickered with Erik, but Jed was in no mood to laugh. His hand gripped the wheel tensely. Chris looked over at Jed and said, "You can stop the car if you need to."

Jed finally just pulled to a stop, out in the middle of nowhere with snow falling at the fastest pace he'd ever seen, even having grown up in northern Minnesota his whole life. "Well, boys, I guess my dad might have been right about the freak storm they were predicting. This is ridiculous, and I can't go any further until it clears up a bit."

The car was quiet. "Maybe we should call someone," suggested Erik, never the brightest bulb in the lamp.

"Well, genius, I can't *see* enough to drive! Do you think a tow truck is coming for us?"

Chris spoke more soothingly, "Don't worry. It'll be fine. We'll just wait the storm out right here."

"But I can't keep the car running because we'll run out of gas," said Jeb, quietly.

"If you don't keep the car running, Jed, we'll freeze," Erik answered.

The boys suddenly realized the weight of the consequences of their decisions and fear descended upon them.

Jed prayed quietly to himself, *God, please help us get out of this mess. I'm sorry I ever doubted my father. And I'm so embarrassed at my arrogance!* Jed realized that even when he thought his parents' rules might be too strict or constricting, they were probably for his own good, to protect him from the dangers he was too young and inexperienced to recognize.

Luckily, about two hours later, the boys, who were all shivering together in the back seat, noticed the snowflakes seemed less impenetrable. The air had cleared just enough, and they could still make out the rough outline of the country road under the snow drifts.

They picked their way carefully back to the highway and drove home with their proverbial tails between their legs.

Even though Jed came in through the garage at 1:30 a.m., his dad was sitting on the living room couch, waiting.

"Did you get stuck in the snow?"

Jed looked at his dad, gauging. He knew that he knew. It was an interesting stand-off. Jed nodded, not giving anything away.

"Well," his father said, "At least you got back home safely. I'm glad."

"Thanks, Dad. You were right to warn me. Thank you," was all Jed said before heading off to bed.

Hymn: *Come, Thou Long Expected Jesus!*
Author: Charles Wesley (1744)
Prayer Songs

1 Come, thou long expected Jesus,
    born to set thy people free;
    from our fears and sins release us,
    let us find our rest in thee.
    Israel's strength and consolation,
    hope of all the earth thou art;
    dear desire of every nation,
    joy of every longing heart.

2 Born thy people to deliver,
    born a child and yet a King,
    born to reign in us forever,
    now thy gracious kingdom bring.
    By thine own eternal spirit

rule in all our hearts alone;
by thine all sufficient merit,
raise us to thy glorious throne.

Prayer

Heavenly Pappa, how I chafe at your good rules! How I struggle at your restraints. And how much patience you always show me! I pray for Your forgiveness and Your grace. Help me see the error in my arrogance and appreciate that Your laws are always meant for my good. Thank You, God, for Your patience and Your providence and provision in my life. Amen.

Discussion Questions:

1. What does freedom in Christ mean to you?

2. How does Jesus bring redemption into our lives?

3. In what areas of your life do you need redemption or freedom?

Christmas Commission

Go ice-skating or simply take a walk in the chilly air. Do something winter-focused as a family, recognizing that God made the spring, summer, fall, and winter. He created *all*.

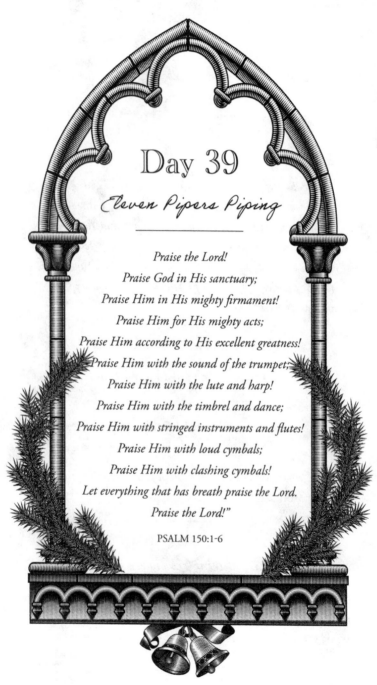

Day 39

Eleven Pipers Piping

Praise the Lord!
Praise God in His sanctuary;
Praise Him in His mighty firmament!
Praise Him for His mighty acts;
Praise Him according to His excellent greatness!
Praise Him with the sound of the trumpet;
Praise Him with the lute and harp!
Praise Him with the timbrel and dance;
Praise Him with stringed instruments and flutes!
Praise Him with loud cymbals;
Praise Him with clashing cymbals!
Let everything that has breath praise the Lord.
Praise the Lord!"

PSALM 150:1-6

Beth was flummoxed. Her boss had just told her she needed to make the presentation at the conference the next day. "My mother-in-law just passed away and I need to fly with my wife to Chicago. Marcus, as you know, is already out of town. You know the product as well as he does, so I have perfect confidence in you. Just work off the slides like we always do."

"Yes, sir. I hope I live up to your expectations." Beth walked back to her office in a daze. She'd never been asked to give a client presentation, much less one in front of an entire room full of conference attendees. It was terribly intimidating. It was his company, his rules, of course, but he always made the presentations and Beth had very little experience speaking in public. That was the one class in high school she absolutely abhorred. She'd earned a C, but only because her teacher had commended her for how hard she had tried. She was certain everyone else had made A's.

She fretted for the rest of the day at work and then went home to her cat and worried some more while she fed Pixie. Finally, she started to think clearly about the tremendous responsibility her boss had just given her—representing their company to the world at large. That made her feel even worse!

Beth needed to get herself under control. *You know what you're doing, Beth, so you just need to share that with the people in the room.* Beth already had the PowerPoint, so that part was finished, but she felt such pressure to be able to speak cogently and authoritatively on the software she had helped develop.

When she got ready for bed, she pulled out her Bible as she always did, and opened it to read. The passage that she pulled up to read was about Solomon asking the Lord for wisdom and receiving it. *Oh, God, please give me also wisdom and ability for tomorrow's presentation,* she prayed silently. Beth went to sleep with that prayer on her lips.

The next morning, Beth arose early and picked out her most powerful-feeling suit, a navy pinstripe with a creamy shell and silk organza scarf with blue forget-me-nots. The scarf had been a gift from her father for achieving her master's, so it imbued her with confidence as she tied it around her neck. She acknowledged to herself she needed all the help she could get.

She sat down to a good breakfast. Well, she made a hearty breakfast, but then barely touched it. She just wasn't hungry. She downed a glass of orange juice, pet Pixie goodbye, and jumped in her car.

The conference was downtown at the convention center, an intimidating complex of large buildings and an imposing parking structure. She drove into it and found a space. *So far, so good!* she thought. She grabbed her bag and briefcase and headed inside, following signs to find the area where she'd be presenting. She checked in with staff, reviewed the AV tech stuff and handed them her thumb drive. Then she entered the large room to look around.

What she saw made her heart skip a beat. There must have been more than five hundred people in the room, all at tables, many of them taking notes. For Beth, *intimidated* didn't even approach the sickness she felt in her stomach. She ran out of the room to find the ladies room and vomited the small amount of breakfast she'd been able to swallow earlier.

Oh, God in heaven! What have I gotten myself into? Please be merciful and deliver me from this accursed assignment! Have Marcus show up! Have my boss return. Cancel his flight! Save me from this, please!

Beth's cell phone rang as she was rinsing her mouth out in the bathroom sink. It was Marcus! Could God have answered her prayers so expediently? Ready for the miracle, she answered confidently, "Beth Masters' phone."

"Beth, it's Marcus. I heard you're making the presentation today. Congratulations!"

"Oh," Beth responded weakly, realizing her mistake. Then she attempted a bit more enthusiasm. "Thanks. It's—uh—gonna be good! Uhm. . . . How's your trip going?"

"Thanks for asking! Really well! I'm getting us some new clients, so we'll be plenty busy next week when I'm back!"

"That's fantastic!"

"Well, I've got to run but, break a leg!" Marcus said and hung up.

Beth looked at herself in the mirror and realized she'd stained her scarf. "Crap!" she said out loud. Someone came out of the stall behind her as she tore the scarf from around her neck and looked around for something to use.

"Did y'all need some help?" the pretty blond woman asked Beth. She was petite and wore stiletto-heeled boots with a short skirt suit. She also had the prettiest make up, impressing Beth.

"Uh . . . I, uhm, just threw up," Beth said, gesturing to the toilet, "and it seems I got some on my scarf."

"Well, Honey, we just need to rinse that right out, lickety-split! If you don't, it's gonna set, you know? Here." She gently took and put the scarf under the faucet, turning it this way and that to let the water run through it. "You can't put this back on, probably, but let's see, here. Look. It's almost clean, now. Lucky you! You caught it in time! I'm Trixie, by the way."

"Oh. Nice to meet you. I'm Beth. Thank you for helping me. I'm supposed to make a presentation and I'm a bit nervous."

Trixie held up the scarf and it looked perfect, though wet.

"You know, I'm happy to lay your scarf out on the chair next to me at the conference, to let it dry, if you're speaking soon. You can't put it back on when it's all wet like this, but it'll dry quick. Look. It's not even dripping anymore. I squeezed all the excess water out of it."

"Well, I suppose that's the best offer I've got. Thank you! You're a Godsend!"

"Sweetie, we better get you back in there before they start looking for you!" said Trixie.

A half-hour of sweating and anxiety later, they announced Beth's boss to the stage. Beth had told them about the substitution, so she assumed a communication breakdown on their end.

Holy spirit, guide my speech. Let me say the words they need to hear. In my weakness, Lord, show your strength. And thank you for Trixie.

Beth walked out onto the vast stage. It seemed to take forever to reach the podium, with the enormous audience tracking her every step. When she got there, she leaned into the mic and said, "I know I don't look like Mr. Buck Wakeman, and I apologize. He was called away on a personal matter and sends his regrets. I'll do my best to fill his shoes this morning."

She didn't remember much after that, but Trixie told her she knocked it out of the park. Trixie would be her first client from the event. Beth knew it was the answer to her prayers and she told Trixie that.

"Honey, there's no doubt that God moves in our lives, all the time. It's just that sometimes, we get the opportunity to really feel His presence. I'm just so honored to have shared that with you, here, today!"

Hymn: *O Come, O Come, Emmanuel*
Translator: J.M. Neale (1851)
Tune: *Veni Emmanuel* (Chant)
Opening Hymns

1   O come, O come, Immanuel,
      and ransom captive Israel
      that mourns in lonely exile here
      until the Son of God appear.

   Refrain:
   Rejoice! Rejoice! Immanuel
   shall come to you, O Israel.

2   O come, O Wisdom from on high,
      who ordered all things mightily;
      to us the path of knowledge show
      and teach us in its ways to go. [*Refrain*]

3 O come, O come, great Lord of might,
   who to your tribes on Sinai's height
   in ancient times did give the law
   in cloud and majesty and awe. [*Refrain*]

4 O come, O Branch of Jesse's stem,
   unto your own and rescue them!
   From depths of hell your people save,
   and give them victory o'er the grave. [*Refrain*]

5 O come, O Key of David, come
   and open wide our heavenly home.
   Make safe for us the heavenward road
   and bar the way to death's abode. [*Refrain*]

6 O come, O Bright and Morning Star,
   and bring us comfort from afar!
   Dispel the shadows of the night
   and turn our darkness into light. [*Refrain*]

7 O come, O King of nations, bind
   in one the hearts of all mankind.
   Bid all our sad divisions cease
   and be yourself our King of Peace. [*Refrain*]

Prayer

Who am I that You care so deeply for me, God? I am Your child. I am Your beloved. You're your cherished creation. Help me to make you proud, Lord, please. Amen.

Discussion Questions

1. How can we worship God in our daily lives?

_____

2. Why is worship essential in our relationship with God?

_____

3. How does praising God impact our perspective on life?

_____

Christmas Commission

Make a game out of trying to work examples of God's goodness in your life into conversations with other people, believers and non-believers alike. Make God proud to call you His own by praising Him to others!

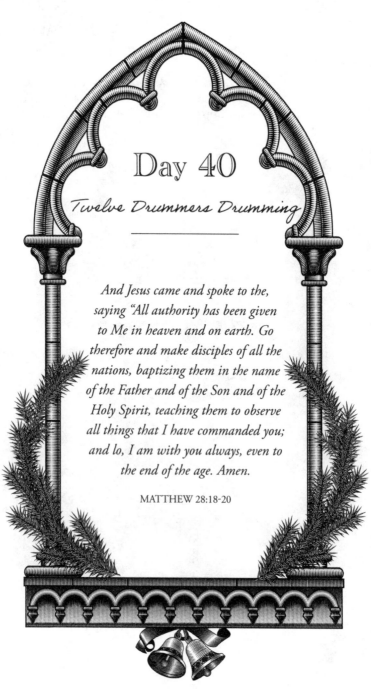

Day 40

Twelve Drummers Drumming

---

*And Jesus came and spoke to the,
saying "All authority has been given
to Me in heaven and on earth. Go
therefore and make disciples of all the
nations, baptizing them in the name
of the Father and of the Son and of the
Holy Spirit, teaching them to observe
all things that I have commanded you;
and lo, I am with you always, even to
the end of the age. Amen.*

MATTHEW 28:18-20

The professor stood in front of his Ethics 101 students. *What is Happiness?* he wrote on the board, under his name: *Professor Radcliff (Call me RAD)*. It was the first day of classes and, because Rad was new to campus his students had little idea what to expect.

"Anyone? What *makes* you happy, for instance?" Rad motioned to the board behind him in expectation.

One bold student raised his hand, and Rad, an evolved, progressive type of guy, smiled and motioned for him to answer. "First, please say your name to the class so we might all get to know each other. As you can see, I've written my name and how you may address me on the board." Some students snickered behind their palms.

"Hi. My name is Benny. Sinking my toes into warm sand makes me happy."

Another student bravely rose her hand. "I'm Josie and fresh-baked chocolate chip cookies make me happy."

"Excellent," said Rad. "See? It's not a trick question. Write on your notepaper this question and five answers, for yourselves. Take a few minutes, but it shouldn't take too long to name five things that make you happy."

He waited while students pondered.

Grant quickly filled in his five top things and put down his pen. He looked around the small theater-styled classroom. The professor stood center stage in front of about thirty-five students.

"Now, please write *why* those things make you happy. We are organizing our thoughts to define happiness—what is it and how do we attain it."

The class dutifully went back to pondering and writing.

"Time's up!" Rad said after a short time. "Now, I want to hear something that makes you happy and why. Go." He pointed to a young woman in the front.

"My boyfriend, because I love him."

The class laughed. The professor nodded and smiled. "You." He pointed at a male hippie-type student with dreads.

"Hanging out on the quad, playing hacky-sack, not doing my schoolwork, because being purposely lazy soothes me."

"Sounds like you've given it some thought, already. And you feel you need soothing?"

"Absolutely."

"Hm. We're going to get along just fine. . . . "

A clean-cut young man in a green T-shirt and jeans chimed in, "But doesn't postponing your work bring any anxiety?"

"Nothing a beer or two won't cure!" the Rastafarian answered.

"You." Rad pointed to the green T-shirt guy.

"Uhm. I'm Heath. Sure, uh, Rad, Jesus Christ makes me happy because He promises eternal life, and that gives me hope. And hope is one of the most important ingredients for happiness."

Rad laughed. "Are you for real? Hope is an ingredient for happiness? In whose recipe?"

"Everyone's," answered Heath. "Did anyone write down money?" He looked around for an answer.

Rad chimed in. "Of course. I'm sure someone in here wrote down a million bucks or winning the lottery, right? Raise your hands. There's no shame!"

About half the class raised their hands. Rad counted them silently as he said, "There. You see, several students wrote down money makes them happy. What of it, Heath?"

"Well, money won't make you happy without hope. If I gave you a million dollars and told you that you were going to die tomorrow, you wouldn't be happy, would you?"

The class was silent, looking around for others' reactions. Dreadlocks guy said quietly, "That's messed up, man."

The professor wasn't so easily subdued. "So, you said hope is important, and then claimed that Jesus gives you hope? Explain."

"The Bible says, '. . . if you confess with your mouth that Jesus is Lord and believe in your heart that God raised Him from the dead, you will be saved.' That gives me hope, because Jesus promises eternal life and, even better, forgiveness for my sins."

Professor Rad paused only for a moment. Then he smiled. "Well, you can believe what you want, but we don't traffic in superstitions in this class, Heath. But you said hope was only one component of happiness. Name another, please."

"Sure. Gratitude."

Rad smiled again, contemplative. "Class, what do you say to that?"

The class responded with chatter, mostly critical.

"Can you offer a solid defense of that point of view?"

"Just that it's the truth. Without a posture of gratitude, there's only entitlement, which boils down to *nothing* ever being good enough—ever being *enough*, full stop. If I get a scholarship I didn't have to work hard to win, and I'm ungrateful, I'm left wondering why I didn't get more money? That's unhappiness."

"You seem to have thought a lot about this. . . . "

"Professor Rad, the culture has forced me to think about this. The message today is *Do what makes you happy!* But just pursuing hedonistic pleasure is ultimately debilitating, because without purpose or gratitude or hope, happiness is circumstantial and fleeting, and we become slaves to the physical. A cookie, warm sand, being lazy . . . no disrespect intended, but those things aren't true happiness, because true happiness is the thing no one can take away. The thing you control entirely yourself. It's even in our founding documents."

"What is?" Rad asked, a bit too quickly.

"Life, liberty, and the pursuit of happiness. That last bit is about pursuing one's purpose, finding out what you are made of, in essence. It's from Aristotle. His definition of happiness would have been *fulfillment of purpose*—the satisfaction that comes from a job well done."

"Mr. Heath! You seem to be confusing *happiness* with *meaning*. In this class, we differentiate between the two. But this was a nice diversion, thank you. Now, let's open our textbooks and get started."

Hymn: *Be Thou My Vision*
Author: Dallan Forgaill
Music: *Slane Hill*

Be Thou my Vision, O Lord of my heart;
Naught be all else to me, save that Thou art;
Thou my best thought, by day or by night,
Waking or sleeping, Thy presence my light.

Be Thou my Wisdom, and Thou my true Word;
I ever with Thee and Thou with me, Lord;
Thou my great Father, and I Thy true son,
Thou in me dwelling, and I with Thee one.

Riches I heed not, nor man's empty praise;
Thou mine inheritance, now and always;
Thou and Thou only, first in my heart,
High King of heaven, my treasure Thou art.

High King of heaven, my victory won,
May I reach heaven's joys, O bright heav'n's Sun!
Heart of my own heart, whatever befall,
Still be my Vision, O Ruler of all.

Prayer

Lord, Your grace is all I need. Your love knows no bounds and lifts me up from where my blunders and my hubris leave me, destitute but for Your intersession. Thank you for coming to my rescue! Let me praise Your name for the rest of my days! Amen.

Discussion Questions:

1. Does your definition of happiness depend on external circumstances?

   _____

2. How does the message of Christ speak to a deeper sense of purpose?

   _____

3. What can we do to share the Gospel with others?

   _____

Christmas Commissions

1. There is no such thing as coincidence. Make a habit of sharing the stories of God's provision in your life with others. Allowing someone else to witness your experience of God working in your life may tempt them to delve further into their own relationship with Him.

2. Consider starting a Bible study, just to read the Word with others and discuss it together, in your home each week. If you wonder where to start, try the book of John, using an annotated Bible.

Afterword

Epiphany

Christians celebrate Epiphany on January 6th, twelve days after Christmas Day. The word means *appearance* or *manifestation*. Around the world, many cultures refer to it as Three Kings Day, naming it after the Magi who visited Christ as a baby. As Gentiles, they illustrate that God intended His gift to the world, not just to the Jews.

Another *epiphany* common to Christians is comprehending that happiness is entirely independent of physical comfort. Remember that childhood Christmas gift that you were just dying to receive? And then, once you got it, how quickly it tarnished or broke, or you simply lost interest?

Like children, we were once victims of our wants and needs, but maturity brings the understanding that cheerfulness is a choice. Paul and Silas sang in their prison cell (Acts 16:25-34), defying worldly expectations. Aleksandr Solzhenitsyn, author of the famous *Gulag Archipelago*, wrote, "Bless you prison, bless you for being in my life. For there, lying upon the rotting prison straw, I came to realize that the object of life is not prosperity as we are made to believe, but the maturity of the human soul." And Boethius came to a similar conclusion in *The Consolation of Philosophy*, which he composed while imprisoned and awaiting his imminent execution for his impeccable integrity. "Has the world become so topsy-turvy that a living creature, whom the gift of reason makes divine, believes that his glory lies solely in possession of lifeless goods?" Boethius concluded that happiness is best won through pursuing virtue or goodness.

Aristotle similarly held that everyone possessed a unique calling—something attuned to the character of that individual. That special gifting indicated the person's reason for being. Therefore, as we are created with purpose, achieving our intention should be the most satisfying thing to accomplish. By Aristotle's measurement, fulfillment of one's purpose was the key to attaining the elusive but enduring happiness we all crave. It is that sentiment our nation's founders enshrined with the phrase "Life, liberty, and the pursuit of happiness."

The great philosophers cautioned us happiness generates from within, distinct from external conditions, which contradicts our current, decreasingly Christian culture. Instagram boasts, *Do what makes you happy!* Bumper stickers advise *Choose happiness.* The famous song says, "Don't worry, be happy." And the culture at large is relatively hedonistic.

If we only did things that made us happy momentarily, we would never clean the dishes or mow the lawn. We do the daily chores to achieve greater enjoyment later, like having a picnic with family on the freshly-mown grass while eating off clean, not filthy, dishes.

While we don't necessarily love to wash dishes, we understand that the pleasure comes from having clean tableware, just like investing in our studies and engaging our minds reaps future rewards. Pursuit of our greater purpose will necessarily bring deeper, more abiding, happiness.

The Christian admonition is to do things that are pleasing to the Lord, and in pleasing Him, find joy. Philippians 4:8-9 reads:

> *Finally, brethren, whatever things*
> *are true, whatever things are noble,*
> *whatever things are just, whatever*
> *things are pure, whatever things are*
> *lovely, whatever things are of good*
> *report, if there is any virtue and if*
> *there is anything praiseworthy—*
> *meditate on these things. The things*
> *which you learned and received and*
> *heard and saw in me, these do, and*
> *the God of peace will be with you.*

We must all discern the animating element of our lives: why are we here? After watching a Shakespeare play at the Guthrie Theater during a fifth-grade school trip in Minneapolis, eleven-year-old Kevin discovered his *raison d'être*, never to waiver. But it was when God diverted him wisth three strokes and compromised his Hollywood acting career that Kevin started to see the fuller meaning for his drive: filming stories to bring fellow souls closer to Christ, thereby improving the culture.

Sam discovered her love for acting in her high school drama class. Her teachers and others scoffed it was pie in the sky, that she was better off studying medicine for a stable job, instead. Modeling to earn college money taught Sam that the advice to focus solely on college was faulty and even deceitful. (Sam was one of two students from her school to achieve success in Hollywood within a few years of graduating.) Now, Sam performs in the *even more fulfilling* roles of wife, mother, and educator, and has allowed her passion to lead her to discover an entirely new purpose, encouraging parents to home-educate and emancipating children from the schools.

Once Kevin and Sam uncovered their vocations (what Christ called them to do here on Earth), things fell into place in ways they cannot fully explain without invoking our supernatural Creator, work fused with pleasure, and they experienced abiding joy.

The secret to happiness is that it doesn't exist, in and of itself. It can only be obtained as a byproduct of pursuing and fulfilling purpose. Although the ancients knew it, our current culture struggles with distraction and perversion and ignores the intention behind every life. We were all *created* for a reason and not evolved from some primordial goo.

Our fervent prayer is for you, dear reader, to find your life's fulfillment and the joy that accompanies it. Fix your eyes on the hope and future eternal you have in Christ Jesus. Be in service of Him who rules the world. Through prayer and introspection, discover His purpose in your life and strive courageously toward it with a joyful heart, knowing that your goal is Christ's accomplishment within you. For, as Boethius counsels us in *Consolation of Philosophy*, "How happy is mankind, if the love that orders the stars above rules, too, in your hearts." Allow His contentment to inhabit you like the warmth of a fresh-baked cookie or a songbird's notes on a warm, sunny morning. That is true happiness.

That is our wish for you, each Christmas and throughout the year.

Hymn: *O Holy Night*
Translator: John S. Dwight
Author: Placide Cappeau (1847)
Tune: *Cantique De Noel*

1   O holy night! the stars are brightly shining;
    It is the night of the dear Savior's birth.
    Long lay the world in sin and error pining,
    Till He appeared and the soul felt its worth.
    A thrill of hope—the weary world rejoices,
    For yonder breaks a new and glorious morn!
    Fall on your knees! O hear the angel voices!
    O night divine, O night when Christ was born!
    O night, O holy night, O night divine!

2   Led by the light of faith serenely beaming,
    With glowing hearts by His cradle we stand.
    So led by light of a star sweetly gleaming,
    Here came the Wise Men from Orient land.
    The King of kings lay thus in lowly manger,
    In all our trials born to be our Friend.
    He knows our need—to our weakness is no stranger.
    Behold your King, before Him lowly bend!
    Behold your King, before Him lowly bend!

3   Truly He taught us to love one another;
    His law is love and His gospel is peace.
    Chains shall He break, for the slave is our brother,

231

And in His name all oppression shall cease.
Sweet hymns of joy in grateful chorus raise we;
Let all within us praise His holy name.
Christ is the Lord! O praise His name forever!
His pow'r and glory evermore proclaim!
His pow'r and glory evermore proclaim

Acknowledgments

A Christian's walk is continually progressing. Many people have met us and journeyed with us both on our way. There are too many to fully recognize in the space allotted here, but let us start with Ardis, Lynn, M.F., and Renée, for their mentorship. Pastor Mark Pickerill, the man who married us. Pastor Rob McCoy, who called us and our children to the cross for over a decade. Our friends who came alongside us in spiritual support during our trials (you know who you are), including Kym, Paul, Peter, Jacquie, and Dr. Phil Stutz, who offered Kevin the grateful prayer as a coping tool when Kevin was at his lowest. Recognizing God in all the little things has been our utmost joy and having others encouraging us and pointing Him out compounded our delight in His ways. We also must acknowledge Keith, without whose encouragement this book would not exist, and Patty, whose dedication to perfection made it all that we'd hoped.

About the Authors

Sam Jenkins met Kevin Sorbo when she performed as a guest star on his internationally acclaimed TV show, *Hercules: The Legendary Journeys*. Theirs was a love affair for the storybooks: lovely, talented starlet meets handsome, charismatic hero who charmingly sweeps her off her feet and she, in return, rescues him, later. Even their first date was  peppered with foreshadowing of their marriage ceremony and the three children they would have, "boy, boy, girl." Although raised by her self-sufficient mother to be an independent, career-focused woman, when Kevin suffered three strokes just prior to their wedding, Sam chose to abandon her career and devote herself in support of his uncertain recovery, leading her to become a strong advocate for traditional values.

After an intense three year battle against debilitating stroke symptoms, Kevin emerged triumphant. He deftly recounts his struggles in *True Strength: My Battle from Hercules to Mere Mortal and How Nearly Dying Saved My Life*. His raw, ernest story has offered many readers solace and encouragement to overcome their own health challenges. Together, the Sorbos wrote their sequel *True Faith: Embracing Adversity to Live in God's Light*, which expounds on the benefits and importance of marriage and living authentically, among other things.

As filmmakers and actors, the Sorbos eagerly collaborate, as they both feel compelled to improve the world using story-telling with film as a powerful vehicle for communicating ideas and values. Their first collaboration as producers was *Let There Be Light*, a film co-written by Sam and directed by Kevin, which ranked second in opening weekend box office against *Thor: Ragnorok*. The film starred both Sorbos and included their boys, Braeden and Shane, plus a cameo from their young daughter, Octavia. It was a film by a family, for families, with true family (i.e., Christian) values at its core and its remarkable success and resonance with the audience established Sorbo Studios. The Sorbo team followed that drama with the acclaimed comedy, *Miracle in East Texas*, which was based on a true story and in which Sam co-starred with Kevin who, once again, also directed.

Because of their devotion to family and to God, the Sorbos chose to home educate their young children. Through this experience, Sam has become the premiere voice for home education, authoring several books and speaking across the country and internationally on behalf of educational freedom and cultural emancipation from schools.

The Sorbos reside in West Palm Beach, Florida.